THE DA...

Chris wants to save the world from nuclear destruction; he wants to escape from the values of his clinging, middle-aged parents; he wants a lifestyle of comradeship and easy sex, and he thinks he has found all this when he joins D.A.M.N.—a group within the peace movement who believe that violence and direct action are more effective than peaceful demonstrations.

But when Chris meets Sarah, she forces him to question whether violence is ever really justified—even when the future of the world is at stake—and he is made to confront not only her pacifism, but also his own conflicting loyalties.

BY THE SAME AUTHOR

Your Friend, Rebecca

THE DAMNED

Linda Hoy

'Those who do evil that good may come shall be damned; for the way of peace have they not known.'

THE BODLEY HEAD
LONDON   SYDNEY
TORONTO

ACKNOWLEDGEMENTS

The lines quoted on pages 21, 67, and 160 are from 'Do Not Go Gentle into that Good Night' from Dylan Thomas's *Collected Poems* published by J. M. Dent and reprinted by permission of David Higham Associates Limited.

This is not a true story. All the characters are imaginary and to the best of my knowledge, there is no such group as *Direct Action against the Missiles Now* at present in existence. The activities of a Direct Action Group, like D.A.M.N., which believes in the use of violence, would not be condoned by the Campaign for Nuclear Disarmament or any other known peace organization. L.H.

British Library Cataloguing in Publication Data

Hoy, Linda
The damned.
I. Title
823'.914 [J]   PR6058.O/

ISBN 0-370-30520-5

© Linda Hoy 1983
Printed and bound in Great Britain for
The Bodley Head Ltd
9 Bow Street, London WC2E 7AL
by Spottiswoode Ballantyne Ltd, Colchester
Set in Linotron 202 Plantin
First published 1983

This book is dedicated to my
many friends and comrades, citizens of
the People's Republic of South Yorkshire,
who are working together for peace.

1

I wish I could screw her. She's very beautiful with long, blonde hair and a body like a film star. When she smiles at me, I lower my eyes. I don't want her to win; that's the thought I keep uppermost in my mind. I want her to feel humiliated.

I sit down at the table and begin to sort out my pieces, trying to keep my eyes averted from her legs. She's wearing a very short skirt and her legs are long and suntanned. On her shirt is pinned a badge that says, *Donna Massey*, *Captain*. Our captain is away this week, and they're taking a gamble putting me against her. I want to prove myself by winning.

Donna sits down at the table, placing her pieces on the board. She stretches out her legs and, when they touch mine, I move instinctively away. It makes me feel uneasy to sit with my legs touching those of a girl as beautiful as she is.

I start to play. My opening moves are harmless, bringing out my knights and bishops so I can move them forward later when I've worked out a plan of attack. I stare at Donna's side of the board, trying to read inside her mind. I need to anticipate every move, every strategy, so that I can keep a step ahead of her, blocking her way forward whenever she formulates a plan. Her moves seem random; nothing links together. I decide she has no strategy and concentrate on arranging my own pieces, moving them into positions where I can bring them forward ready for the kill.

I become increasingly conscious of Donna's legs. The vibrations I felt when we made contact have radically disturbed my body chemistry. I find myself moving my left leg very, very slowly over in her direction. I want to touch her again.

I focus my mind on the board where Donna has shifted out her queen, but I can't see any motive, any danger. It's as if the table is made of glass and all I can see, when I gaze down at the board, are Donna's long and suntanned thighs stretched out lazily only a minute distance from my knee.

I move my white knight forward in line with her queen and then concentrate on easing my knee slowly and deliberately over towards her leg. My knee makes contact. The touch is so gentle and tentative that I think she hasn't noticed, but I feel sensations shooting upwards through my thigh with an intensity that forces me to grip the table for support. I shift about awkwardly in my seat, then place my hand inside my trouser pocket and fumble around to try and make myself more comfortable. I move nearer to the table to hide the lower part of my anatomy from view. I don't want anyone to notice the physical effect this scene is having on me.

Donna moves her queen down towards my knight. I study the board again to check I'm not being threatened and slowly the realization comes to me that Donna has made a mistake, a big mistake: I can take her queen with my pawn. The excitement in me grows as I sense quite suddenly that I'm going to win this game. If a girl can make mistakes like that, then thrashing her will be easy, a push-over. I don't want her to see the excitement register on my face. I have to keep the mask on, calm and cool—try to keep my face a blank. But secretly, I start to relish the power of winning. Donna thinks I'm easy; she thinks she needn't work too hard with me. But she's wrong. I'm not easy. I'm a good chess-player and I play a hard game. Nobody walks over Chris Fieldsend.

I reach out leisurely and take her queen with my pawn, then I loll back in my chair a little and relax, watching her eyes intently. I like watching other people know they're beaten.

Donna's face is impassive. First of all, she moves her leg away from me beneath the table. She moves it quite decisively as if maybe she'd been aware all the time that it was keeping me distracted. Then she glances at me straight between the eyes; it isn't the look a person gives you when they know they're beaten. I start to feel uneasy.

Donna picks up her castle. She moves it quickly, in a way that makes it obvious that her moves are pre-determined, thought-out, planned. I feel a sinking in my stomach as I realize that I've walked into an ambush. Donna's moves have been calculated in advance, weaving a trap round me, offering me her queen, her best piece, as a lure. I start to feel humiliated.

Donna takes my pawn with her castle, placing it coolly in direct line with my king. She glances up at me and her face has the faint suggestion of a smile. 'Checkmate,' she says quietly.

I gaze down at the board, at my king trapped tightly between her knight, her bishop and her castle and held in place by my own pawns—pieces I could have moved away, if I'd been quick enough to suss her out. I look at my knights and bishops standing to attention on the centre of the board, waiting for the orders to carry out the plan that I hadn't got round to thinking of. I close my eyes for a moment. I wish I could disintegrate, beam off to a distant planet like an alien from 'Star Trek'.

I want to look cool and calm. I don't want her to see the disappointment in my face. I open my eyes and force myself to smile at her. I want to think of something clever and witty to say to spoil her moment of triumph, but the words clog up like a ball of plasticine inside my throat. I nod slowly at her, accepting the result.

The other kids in the team commiserate with me as they pick up their coats and head for the door. I shrug my shoulders as if defeat means nothing, but the weight still lingers like a lump of granite in my guts.

Helen Wheatley corners me before I can sidle out through the door. On a good day, Helen Wheatley is a pain; at a time like this she's agony. 'Can we give you a lift home, Chris?' she asks me, giggling. Helen giggles all the time. 'Daddy's brought the Rover; we can drop you off.' She gazes up at me with admiration slithering down her cheek-bones. It makes no difference to Helen whether I win a match or not. She'd still worship the ground I walked on, if I turned into a slimy frog covered in warts and pond gunge. Ground I hopped on, perhaps I ought to say. We call her the chess team groupie.

'I was going to catch the bus,' I tell her. Helen glances at her fancy gold watch. 'You've just missed it,' she tells me cheerfully. 'And it's pouring down with rain . . .'

I haven't brought a coat and I don't fancy swimming home. I look up at Helen and I shrug my shoulders. 'O.K.,' I tell her.

'Hello there!' Mr Wheatley beams at us as he opens the car door. 'Did you have a good match?'

I mutter something inaudible. Lee Furgusson's coming with us and he won his game, so he says, 'Yeah. Great!' to Mr Wheatley, as he stands aside like a gentleman to let Helen in the car first. Then he quickly side-steps and tries to shove me in beside her. It's a standard joke amongst the kids about how much Helen fancies me and they're always trying to shove the two of us together. I'd rather sit in a car next to a dried-up turtle than sit with Helen Wheatley. I stand aside, discreetly place my weight on the toe of Lee's shoe, then twist his arm behind his back and manoeuvre him into the back seat of the car. Lee's face screws up in pain as he collapses on the plush upholstery next to Helen. I grin at him as I go and sit in the front seat next to her father.

'Whereabouts do you live?' he asks me.

'Hagg Farm Lane,' I tell him. 'You can leave me at the bottom of the road.' I don't like people driving me right up to the front door, even when it's raining. I'd rather walk down my own street by myself.

We set off. I turn to look at Lee who's taken his shoe off and is massaging his toe. Helen's just staring out of the window like a plastic doll. When Lee looks up, I make a werewolf face in Helen's direction. Then I hold my nose; the whole car reeks of Helen's perfume. Lee has to hold his face to stop himself from laughing. At least Lee's got a sense of humour—which is more than you can say for Helen Wheatley. When you say things to her like: 'What perfume is it today, Helen—pulverised stale socks? Essence of skunk juice?' she just stares at you in bewilderment.

Actually, Helen's not bad-looking. She doesn't have three heads or anything. She's got two arms and two legs and all the other bits girls are supposed to have, and most of the kids don't understand why I can't force myself to go out with her. The reason is that I know exactly what Helen Wheatley's after and, believe it or not, it isn't what you're thinking. Helen likes to look immaculate. She likes to have nail varnish in the same garish shade as her lipstick; she carries a shoulder-bag in the same slime-green as her shoes. The only thing she lacks that would make the image perfect is an escort—someone to dangle on the end of her arm like a plastic pixie. She wants a kid with creases in his jeans, who doesn't mind smelling like a squashed skunk every time he kisses her good-night—a kid who'll trot beside her pony when she goes riding on a Saturday afternoon.

And I don't want to be a plastic pixie. I don't even feel excited at the thought of kissing her greasy red lips good-night. The only thing I care about is finding a girl that I can screw.

'Here we are, then.' Mr Wheatley pulls up the car at the end of our road and I say thank you very much and climb out. Helen flutters her eyelashes and waves frantically at me through the back window. I try to pretend I haven't seen her as I turn and start to walk up Hagg Farm Lane.

The reason why I don't want taking to the door is because I come from a home that's completely overrun with gnomes—garden gnomes. Not only gnomes but wishing-wells, windmills and polka-dot mushrooms. I can't bear anyone I know to see them.

There's a dumpy little dwarf called Dopey who trundles round the rockery with a wheelbarrowful of bird droppings; there's Wishful Willy staring hopefully into his wishing-well, hypnotized by the dried-up slugs on the bottom; there's Bashful with his little fishing-rod, angling for four hundred years without catching so much as a tadpole.

There's only one interesting thing that's ever happened to the garden gnomes and that was when I was about ten years old and they started tottering round the garden in the middle of the night. This was an important landmark to me, the week of the walkabout gnomes, because it also marked the beginning of my education about the facts of life. This is how it happened.

We looked out of the window one morning and found Sneezy and Snow White roly-polying in the middle of the lawn. I was just mildly curious about how they got there, but my father was furious. He stormed straight out of the back door, ranting on about vandalism and obscenity and *is nothing sacred nowadays*? And he stuck them straight back up again in their proper places at opposite corners of the flower-bed. We thought that would be the last of it, but the next day it was Grumpy and Doc rolling round the rockery, only Grumpy was pointing the other way round and my father was more furious than ever. He told my mother not to look whilst he strode outside and separated them, then he phoned up the local builders' merchant and asked them to send round a pile of ready-mixed concrete. He'd soon put a stop to somebody's little games, he said, and muttered again about hooligans and how youngsters wouldn't have known about such things in his day.

I couldn't see what he meant, nor could I work out what was wrong with Grumpy and Doc rolling round the rockery together, but the following morning my mind was blown completely because there, in the garden, all of them were at it—back-to-front and side-by-side, balancing on the polka-dot mushrooms and swinging upside down from the sails of Grumpy's windmill. A pink bunny rabbit was involved in the orgy somewhere—I can't just remember where—but I do remember what Snow White was doing with Bashful's little fishing-rod and that certainly aroused my curiosity.

My father's ears turned scarlet and he looked as if he was going to have a heart attack. He insisted on my mother and me staying indoors whilst he stormed around the garden, scooping up armfuls of gnomes and toadstools and stomping across to the garage, where he padlocked them safely inside.

The following day, the ready-mixed concrete arrived. The gnomes were taken out of the garage one at a time and plonked back in their separate places, embedded for eternity in thirteen centimetres of super-hard quality concrete. No more fun and games, little gnomes.

That short episode marked the conclusion of the garden gnomes' forays into the field of sex education; for me it was only the beginning.

2

I turn and walk down the driveway, trying not to look at the gnome-filled garden on my right. On my left, under the carport, sits my father's five-gear G.T. San Marino with its caviar-cloth seat trim, front hockey-stick armrests, wheel-embellishers, illuminated front ashtray and remote-control electric windows.

The repayments on the car are so expensive that my dad can hardly afford the petrol to take it on the road. He gives me driving lessons once or twice a month and occasionally uses it for work. He spends his Sundays polishing the chromework and my mother keeps herself busy knitting it little accessories like a steering-wheel glove and a monogrammed gear-stick cover. She made that with the leftovers from the pink furry stuff she used for knitting our bath- and pedestal-mats and bog seat covers, but we don't have monograms on those.

*

It's Monday, so we'll be having cottage pie. That's how my mother is: roast on Sunday, cottage pie on Monday, liver and bacon Tuesday . . . everything has to fit with the routine. Then on Saturday, when she goes shopping at the Co-op, she can buy the same things every week. I just pray that, if I marry, it'll be someone who dares to make pizza or chop suey once or twice a year. It isn't that I don't like my mother. It's just that she's old and rather dim and her mind trundles along on tracks that got covered in rust somewhere around the middle of the eighteenth century. She probably won't ask about the chess game. She doesn't even know how to play. Chess to her is just a freakish way of playing draughts where some of the pieces can move sideways.

I open the door and walk into the steamy kitchen. The cottage pie smells just about ready and my mum is busy stirring gravy. 'Hello,' she says to me. 'Have you been to the band practice?'

I left the school band six months ago, just after Helen Wheatley joined the ranks of the second trombones.

'I had a chess match,' I tell her. 'Don't you remember?' I'd love to have a mother who was young and lively and aware of what was happening in the world.

She tips the gravy into a gravy-boat, an old-fashioned china one that used to belong to her mother. 'How did you get on, then?' she asks me. The apathy in her voice demonstrates that nothing can compete with gravy-stirring to capture her attention at the moment. As I say, my mother has no idea of what's involved in a game of chess. The only game she's ever been known to play is Happy Families.

'We lost,' I tell her, sitting down and pouring myself a cup of tea.

'Oh dear,' she says. Her voice has the same ring of

involvement as it had the day I gave her the raffia pipe-cleaner holder it had taken me eight months to make in infant school. My mother never has smoked a pipe.

I try not to sigh too deeply as I start to eat my cottage pie.

After dinner I go upstairs and do my homework. That doesn't take too long. Then I spend some time looking through my wardrobe. I'm going to a peace group meeting and there's a girl there called Julie, who I'm hoping to impress. She's the Secretary of the group.

Expecting to find good clothes inside my wardrobe is like hoping to hear a rock band at a funeral. You'd see more exciting clothes around at an undertakers' reunion. It's my mother's fault. I keep explaining to her how I only want to wear clothes that I've chosen myself, but it's like trying to communicate with a fossilized stegosaurus. She thinks we're living in the Ice Age. She spends most of her spare time knitting, and my wardrobe's full of hand-knitted sweaters in putrid shades of brown and purple. She got a pattern once at Christmas for a jumper with a reindeer on the front; mine came out like a hyena with a clothes-horse on its head. I've only worn it once.

I mentioned the other week about some fantastic jeans I'd seen in town, hoping that she'd give me the cash to buy them at the week-end. You can guess what happened: she was trotting round the Co-op with her trolley the day after—it was treble saving stamps as well—and they had these kind of reject elephant-warmers—you know, the kind of thing you could fit a pair of woolly mammoths inside, and they'd still have room to dance a Highland Fling. When she produced them out of her shopping basket that night, I glared at them as if they were made out of second-hand bog paper.

'You'll grow into them, Christopher,' my mother said.

She never takes anything back. She's afraid that the Co-op cashiers might lynch her. Even if I changed into the Incredible Hulk, the jeans would still be hanging round my backside like an army surplus tent. I said nothing and hung them up in my wardrobe. I'll try them on again when I'm sixty-three. Army tents might be fashionable by then.

I finish up wearing my oldest jeans. They're faded and patched, but at least they make contact with my skin. I comb my hair in the mirror and practise giving myself a sexy smile. I'll have to win Julie round with charm and personality and hope she's not too bothered about my clothes.

Talking of girls, perhaps there's a few things I ought to explain about myself. The main one is that I don't go in for dating. Helen Wheatley may be an exception in that she has this mad fixation on me, but basically she's typical of the girls you come across in our school. They all want dates and romance and kids that take them to the pictures or walk around the housing estate with them, arm-in-arm. All they talk about is who people are going out with and who they've just packed up. I don't want to mess around like that. Taking out a girl to admire the garden sprinklers and polystyrene Greek urns on our super-duper new housing estate just sounds to me like one big waste of time. As I said before, the only thing I want to find is a girl that I can screw—and I want that pretty badly. You could say that I'm saving myself. All I know is that if I have to save myself much longer, I'll be in danger of exploding round the edges.

The other thing I ought to mention is that I may be inexperienced, but that doesn't mean I'm not prepared. Each time I go to the library—that's once every couple of weeks—I read another chapter in one of those sex manuals that they've got. They're not called sex manuals, by the way, if you're thinking of looking them up; they're called things like *Making it Good* and *Coming Together*, and they come under section 612.6 of the Dewey classification system. Sometimes they keep them in reserve stock and you have to fill in a little card and ask the librarian to find the book for you. It's just the first time that it's embarrassing. I waited until no one was about, then walked over to the counter and handed in my card. I thought the librarian would say I was too young or ask me in a loud voice why I wanted such a dirty book, but she just smiled at me politely and only looked a little bit shocked. I had thought of telling her that I needed the book for a project we were doing in Health Education, but I didn't have to bother. She was very nice about it. It's a good job because, like I say, she had to get the same book out for me six weeks running.

So, over the past few months or so, I've read through all the relevant volumes and I'm now equipped to tell you about every stage of making love, from turning down the lights to saying, 'Thank you; that was fantastic,' when it's all over. I know about VD and contraception and what to do to make a girl excited and what not to do because it might put her off. On paper, I must be one of the world's best teenage lovers. In fact, if they let me take my Sixteen-Plus in Sex, I'd come out with at least one hundred per cent. The only problem is, at the moment, that all this expertise is being wasted. The talent's there, as my trombone teacher used to tell me, it just needs to be brought out into play. I'm just waiting for the kind of girls to come along who know how to appreciate my finer points and, as I may have mentioned before, I do have plenty of them. The girls round where I live just don't know what they're missing.

*

I wrap myself in my Co-op anorak and go downstairs, heading for the door.

My father's just walking through the hall. 'Are you going out?' he asks me. He says it with such amazement in his voice you'd think we were living in a top security mental hospital. There are times when I wonder if we are.

'I'm off down to the Ryecroft peace group,' I explain. 'I told you about it last week.'

He sighs and looks about ninety-four years old. My father used to be in the army, so he doesn't think much of the peace movement. 'I told you last time, Christopher,' he grumbles, sucking on his pipe, 'we don't want you to get involved with things like that. There'll be communists and liberals and all kinds of strange types at those sort of meetings . . .'

When my father talks about 'liberals' he means the free-thinking, imaginative sort of people who might be tempted to roller-skate inside your garden in the middle of the night and demonstrate to your garden gnomes how to get more enjoyment out of life.

'I'll be careful,' I tell him.

'. . . I don't know why you had to leave the Boy Scouts . . .'

If my father had his way, I'd have stayed in the Boy Scouts until I was drawing my old-age pension. I just stand with my hand resting patiently on the door handle.

'. . . or the Woodcraft Folk . . .'

Oh no, not the Woodcraft Folk again. I can't stand it. 'I won't be late back,' is all I say to him as I turn and walk out of the door.

I run down to the bus-stop with the hood up on my anorak, trying to keep out the rain. I hate the anorak. It has this strip of gerbil-skin around the pixie hood that makes me look like an anaemic ferret peering out of a rabbit-hole. I'm just in time to catch the bus for Ryecroft and I climb on and pay my fare and find a seat by myself at the front of the bus. I like sitting on my own.

I've only been to one meeting of the peace group before now and that was to see a film they were showing called *The War Game*. The film was old and black-and-white and crackly, and it broke down twice whilst they were running it. It showed you what the effects would be if a nuclear bomb was dropped on a place in Britain and it made me feel absolutely horrified. I couldn't understand why nobody'd told me about anything like that before. At school we have Health Education and they tell you things like how you've got to brush your teeth at night before you go to bed and wear sensible Co-op sandals so your toes don't all get squashed. They never tell you what to do when your eyeballs melt from heatblast and start slithering down your cheek-bones, or how to avoid waking up one morning inside a five-mile wide bomb crater. They just act as if things like that could never happen.

When I arrived back home from seeing the film, I felt terrible. My mum and dad were staring at ballroom dancing on the goggle-box, like a pair of turtles in a trance. 'There's four thousand sequins on that dress,' my mother exclaimed in amazement as a woman who looked as if she'd escaped from the top of a Christmas tree came whizzing across the screen.

I wanted to tell them how I'd just discovered that the world was about to be blown up.

'And she sewed all those sequins on by herself . . .'

I thought of different ways to introduce the subject into the conversation, but nothing seemed appropriate. The two of them were wrapped up cosily in a little private world, where the only possible hazards were lumps appearing in the gravy and garden gnomes reaching puberty in the middle of the night. How could I break through the sticky cocoon and tell them that the sequined dresses, gravy lumps and garden gnomes were about to shatter into a billion tiny fragments and hurtle through our housing estate like supersonic confetti? I clasped my hands around my cup of tea and gazed in silence at the chocolate-box fairies zooping across the screen. I started to think about a poem we'd been reading in English that day at school. It was by a Welshman called Dylan Thomas. I don't know if you've come across it. It goes:

> 'Do not go gentle into that good night . . .
> Rage, rage against the dying of the light . . .'

My mum and dad went gently, tiptoeing down little pixie paths, oblivious of the nasty giants and big, bad wolves crouching round the corners waiting for them. There was no other way for them but going gently. They would never protest or rebel because that would mean facing up to what was happening in the great big world outside their pixie patch. The house would have to collapse in tiny pieces round their carpet slippers before they'd notice that, whilst they'd been hypnotized by sequins, skipping fairies and pink netting, the world had disappeared.

I don't know where things went wrong with me. I don't know how I came to be born without the ready-tinted contact lenses, cotton wool scream-squasher and nuclear-hazard welcome mat that the rest of the family were fitted with as standard equipment, but I do know that I wasn't born to take things gently. Like it says in the poem, I think I must have been born to rage—rage against the dying of the light. Going gently, I suppose, is easy; it's warm and soft and comfortable. Rage is something hard and cold, and I think I've avoided it so far.

3

The meeting is in an upstairs room at The Black Bull. Already, the room is thick with smoke and there are twenty or thirty people sitting round. Some of the faces look familiar from last week when I came to see the film.

Julie's sitting at a crowded table near the door. When she looks up and sees me, she smiles and motions me to an empty seat beside her. Lovely. I walk across. There are three blokes sitting opposite who look a bit older than Julie and me.

'This is Chris,' Julie tells them. 'He came for the first time last week—to see the film.'

They all smile and nod and say hello, and I pull out the stool at the side of Julie and sit down.

Perhaps I'd better tell you about Julie. She's slim with short, straight hair and heavy eye make-up. She has a thin, boyish kind of face. Her jeans look older than mine—kind of trampled on and lived-in and covered in patches. My father wouldn't let the neighbours see him using jeans like that as an oil rag for the car. She has black, calf-length boots with low heels—not fashionable ones like most girls wear, but the sort that make you wonder whether she's left a motorbike parked outside. She has a faded denim shirt that isn't fastened and, underneath it, she's wearing a plain black T-shirt. I can't help noticing the fact that she doesn't wear a bra. The cotton material falls softly round the shape of her breasts. I hope I'm going to make out with her. I think I am.

'We'd better get some drinks in.' The bloke sitting opposite Julie takes out his wallet and extracts a couple of pound notes. 'Another pint?' he asks people round the table.

'I'll have a half, thanks, Ralph,' Julie tells him.

'Chris?'

You might find it hard to believe this, but tonight is the first time I've ever been inside a pub and I don't want to show myself up by looking ignorant. All we ever drink at home, apart from fifty cups of tea a week, is half a bottle of sherry every Christmas. I decide I'd better play safe and ask for the same as Julie. 'Thanks,' I tell him. 'I'll have a half.'

Ralph goes down to buy the drinks and the meeting gets under way. During the first few items I sit, looking people over. There are students, old-age pensioners, blokes in their working clothes—all sorts of people. Lots of them are wearing badges that say things like, *Warning: H.M. Government is a danger to your health* and *Once you've seen one nuclear war you've seen them all*. But the people sitting at my table are all wearing the same sort of badge. It has a smashed-in-half missile being trampled by a heavy boot, and across the top it has the initials: D.A.M.N.

I don't want Julie to think I'm stupid, but I do want to get talking to her. I lean across and ask her, 'What does D.A.M.N. stand for?', pointing to the badge that she's wearing on her denim shirt.

Julie reaches inside her shoulder-bag and takes out a leaflet. I skim through it, looking at the headings:

THE NUCLEAR THREAT
WHY MARCHES ARE NOT ENOUGH
PREPARE FOR CONFLICT
HOW TO DEAL WITH PACIFIST WETS
DIRECT ACTION AGAINST THE MISSILES NOW!!!

I scan through some of the small print until I get the picture. I don't feel as though I agree with all it says, but I don't want to get into an argument with Julie. I fold up the leaflet and place it in my pocket, as Ralph reappears beside us with the drinks.

I pass Julie's glass across to her, allowing my little finger to touch her hand for about a twentieth of a second. I don't know if she notices or not. Ralph places my beer beside me. 'Thanks,' I tell him.

Julie smiles at me and raises her glass. 'Cheers,' she says.

'Cheers.' I take a sip of the beer. It tastes revolting. I look across at Julie who's swilling hers down her throat like bath-water pouring down a plug-hole and I keep the smile fixed on my face as I force the liquid down my gullet. I can't understand why anybody wants to drink stuff that tastes so foul. I don't know how I'm going to finish it.

'We need lots of helpers for the jumble sale,' the Chairman's saying. 'We've got to raise more cash to pay for publicity for the demo. Can we have some volunteers for helping on the stalls?'

A few people raise their hands and I offer my services as well. I've never helped at a jumble sale—it might be a bit of a laugh, I suppose. I notice that nobody else at our table is offering, but perhaps they're busy on Saturdays.

'O.K.,' says Stewart. He's the Chairman. 'If anybody doesn't know where the church hall is, if they see me afterwards, I'll explain. Now, about the demo . . .'

He goes on to talk about the demonstration that's being held in three or four weeks' time. I'm surprised how complicated it is to organize. When I've seen demonstrations on the television, I've always assumed they were more or less spontaneous. It's not like that at all. They have to plan a route and let the police know how many people they're expecting. The group have had posters and leaflets printed, and they've hired the Civic Hall for a massive rally afterwards. It sounds really good.

Whilst Stewart's talking, I ease my stool across so that I'm sitting as near to Julie as I can. I think about making some big gesture like putting my arm around her waist —that's the kind of thing kids at school do when they're on the make—about four and a half weeks of gestures like that earns you the right to pay for a girl to go to the pictures with you—yuk! The bomb could have dropped by then. I raise my hand towards her then let it fall back by my side. I can't decide if it's the right thing to do or not.

Stewart's going on about the speakers for the rally. There's a boy about my age called Wayne, who'll speak, there's Bev Barnforth who's the local M.P., there's the bishop, a Communist shop steward and somebody from the women's movement. The bloke opposite me, sitting next to Ralph, puts up his hand to speak. I think that Stewart's seen him, but he doesn't take any notice.

After a couple of minutes, this bloke stands up. 'I'd like to say something . . .' he calls out.

'O.K., Mike.' Stewart stops talking and scowls at him.

Mike's voice is very loud and forceful. 'I would like to

inform this meeting,' he starts off, 'that our Direct Action Group have offered a speaker for the rally.'

The other people sitting round our table nod and shout, 'Hear, hear,' and things. I just concentrate on trying to drink my beer. Mike's nearly finished his pint already. At the rate I'm going, I'll have to come back tomorrow night to finish my first glass.

'We've had speeches at every public meeting,' Mike goes on, 'from all sorts of different people. There's not been one meeting so far where we've been allowed a speaker. Ralph here is supposed to be Vice-Chairman of this peace group. I think he ought to be one of the speakers at the rally.'

Mike sits down and lights a cigarette. I notice that his hand is shaking slightly and his jaw is set hard, as if his teeth are clenched together. People start muttering amongst themselves, glaring at Mike as if he's something on the wrong end of a ballistic missile. I don't see why they shouldn't want Ralph to speak, though. It doesn't seem fair if all the other people are represented.

Julie turns to face me. 'It's true,' she explains. 'We do all the work and they never let us have a speaker.'

I nod my head in commiseration. 'That's not right,' I tell her. Whatever it is she believes in, I want her to know that I'm sympathetic.

Stewart's voice breaks through the conversation. 'This item has been discussed before,' he tells everyone. 'At the committee meeting on July twenty-third we took a vote on whether or not to allow a Direct Action Group speaker at the rally.' He pauses, waiting for people to stop muttering amongst themselves. 'The motion was heavily defeated. I've got it here in the minutes . . .'

There are murmurs of agreement from people who must have been present at the meeting.

'You didn't vote on any other speaker,' Julie suddenly shouts out. Her face is animated—not angry like Mike's, but very intense. I realize that this Action Group is something very important to them.

'If we'd voted on whether we wanted that bishop or the trade union bloke to speak, they might not have got a majority. It's not democratic to vote on one speaker and not any others.'

When Julie stops talking, Ralph reaches across and squeezes her arm. 'Very good,' he tells her. He speaks to her rather like a teacher talking to a kid at school.

Julie smiles at him; she doesn't seem to mind being spoken to like that. I wish I could think of something to say to her, something complimentary that would make it seem quite natural for me to put my arm across her shoulders and hug her, but I can't think of anything. I drink some more of the beer.

I look across at Mike, who's tearing an empty cigarette packet into shreds and dropping the pieces on to the floor. His eyes are blazing. Suddenly, he jumps to his feet and bangs down his empty beer mug on the table. 'Can I just ask for one reason . . .' he snarls . . . 'one reason why a member of our organization should not be allowed to speak at the rally?' He glares challengingly about the room before sitting down.

Ralph places his hand tentatively on the shoulder of Mike's leather jacket, but Mike shrugs his hand away and shakes his head.

Then, a little old lady at the other side of the room stands up. She's very thin and frail with tiny legs that look as brittle as a blackbird's. On her head she's wearing what appears to be a dead squirrel with a bunch of cherries in its ear. She has a dead fox slung around her neck and a coat that looks like twenty aardvarks sewn together. On the nose of one of the aardvarks is a cat-shaped badge that says, *Animal Lovers against the Bomb*.

'Do you mind if I speak, Mr Chairman?' she asks Stewart. Her voice sounds like a budgie's with a frog in its throat.

'Go ahead, Miss Meadows,' Stewart tells her.

I'm still trying to sort out about the badge. Perhaps she walks around wearing all her dead pets because she can't bear to bury them in the garden.

'The reason we do not want these people speaking at the rally,' she croaks, 'is because, unlike the other speakers we've invited, their views do not represent the opinions of other members of the Ryecroft peace group.' She pauses and coughs as if there's some kind of blockage in her larynx. Inhaling bits of dead animals all day long must be as harmful for your lungs as smoking seven or eight pipefuls of tobacco. 'They preach violence and intolerance, and we do not want any confusion to arise in the minds of the public between their views and our own.'

Miss Meadows sits down and there's a general nod of agreement around the room. But, before anyone has a chance to say anything, Mike swears at her. He doesn't just swear quietly so that only the people sitting round about can hear, but snarls across the room the most foul profanity that anyone can think of. Even I feel quite embarrassed.

There's a shocked, stunned silence for a few seconds, then Stewart stands up again and says very calmly and politely: 'Thank you, Mike. That explains quite effectively why we don't want any of your organization to speak on our behalf.' He turns to Miss Meadows and apologizes to her, explaining that he knows Mike won't have the decency to apologize himself. Then he continues with the next item on the agenda.

I don't quite know what to make of it all. I want to help with the peace movement and I don't really want to get involved with a group that nobody else agrees with. On the other hand, I like the way they accept me as part of the group and the fact that they've bought me a drink without anybody asking if I'm old enough. I just wish I'd had the sense to ask for shandy.

'I think it's time for my round.' The other bloke sitting next to Mike stands up and starts taking orders. He's really massive with enormous shoulders and a big, square head like Frankenstein's monster. Everybody else has finished their drinks by now, but I've still got half a glassful left. 'No thanks,' I say, when he asks me what I'm drinking. 'I'm O.K.'

'Can't you manage another half?'

I smile and shake my head. I'm relieved when he doesn't insist on my having another drink. He doesn't look the sort of bloke to argue with. Getting on the wrong side of him could be as healthy as taking cuttings from a Triffid.

'I'll have another half, Trevor,' says Julie.

I pass her glass across and Julie turns round and smiles at me. I think I'm getting on O.K. with her. We haven't spoken to each other much but I'm sitting very close to her and she hasn't moved away yet.

When the meeting's finished, people start packing up and moving off downstairs. 'Are you coming down to the bar?' Julie asks me. She puts her head on one side and gives me this beautiful sexy look. I just hope I'm not mistaken when I think she fancies me.

I smile back at her. 'I want to have a word with Stewart about the jumble sale,' I explain. 'I'll come down in a minute.'

'O.K. We'll get you another half in.'

Oh no! I've only just managed to get the first one down. Still, I don't want to miss the chance to sit and chat with her downstairs.

'Thanks. I'll see you later,' I tell her.

Stewart explains to me about the jumble sale and I tell him I'll be there on Saturday at two o'clock. I'm just turning to go, when he looks up at me again and adds, 'Don't let yourself get conned into joining D.A.M.N., Chris.'

I don't think of myself as the sort of person to get conned. I think I'm capable of making my own mind up about things. I just nod at Stewart to make it look as if I understand about it all.

'They're a right load of head-cases,' he tells me.

I don't like to mention that I want to be off because the load of head-cases have half a pint of best bitter waiting for me downstairs.

'It's not that there's anything wrong with Direct Action,' Stewart explains. 'We had a big Non-Violent Direct Action campaign last year at one of the missile bases. But D.A.M.N. are just a pain in the backside. Still,' he says, 'I suppose you've noticed that yourself. You don't need me to tell you.'

He's nearly as bad as my father. He'll be warning me about liberals and communists next.

'I'll be careful,' I tell him as I turn to go downstairs.

4

'Would you like to buy a newspaper?' Ralph asks me, as I sit down next to Julie and pick up the beer they've bought for me.

'O.K.' I pull some loose change out of my pocket and buy a copy of *Action*. 'Is it any good?' I ask Julie.

'It's brilliant.' She opens up the newspaper and points out some of the articles showing scenes of riots and fights with the police. I'm still not sure whether I want to get involved with things like that, but I try to look enthusiastic as I sit close beside her. Our faces are almost touching as we scrutinize the paper.

Across the table from us, Ralph and Mike are still talking about the meeting. 'It's no use losing your temper,' Ralph's explaining to Mike. 'People just switch off. They don't listen to your argument.'

Mike lights up a cigarette and then starts tearing the match to pieces. I don't know what a psychoanalyst would say about him. 'At least I tell them what I think,' he says to Ralph. 'I don't just sit there and listen to all their bloody crap and say nothing.'

Ralph takes a long swig of his beer. 'It might be better sometimes if you did,' he tells him.

There's an uncomfortable silence after that. I take a few gulps of my beer and then ask Julie whereabouts she lives. I'm really pleased when she tells me that she's got a place of her own. All I need to do now is to invite myself round there—like on a Saturday afternoon or something. I'll be well away. I think again about putting my arm around her.

It's not easy. I always thought that drinking beer was supposed to make you lose your inhibitions. If it does, I wish that it would hurry up and take effect. I place my hand on the back of her stool. It isn't exactly touching her, but it would be if she leaned back a bit.

'Have you got a flat?' she asks me.

Have I got a flat? It's like asking my mother if she's got a recipe for fried octopus and rice. 'I wish I had,' I tell her as if that's some compensation. 'It'd be great to live on my own.'

Julie has taken her shirt off and I'm finding it very hard not to stare at her T-shirt. I don't want her to think I've never seen the shape of a female body before. I just allow myself to ogle whenever she turns the other way.

We talk some more and I know that, if I'm going to make some move with Julie, I've got to make it soon. I'll have to be leaving before long to catch the bus back home. I try to look discreetly at my watch, but it's one of those where you have to press a button to make the numbers light up and Julie notices. 'You don't have to go home yet, do you?' she asks me. Her voice is kind of warm and inviting.

I nod. 'Another five minutes.' I try to communicate with the tone of my voice just how much I'd rather stay here with her. I drink some more of the beer. I'm still not halfway down the glass, but everyone else has nearly finished theirs and they're on pints.

Then, quite suddenly, Julie reaches over and places her hand gently on top of mine. I freeze. I try to keep myself relaxed, but it's as if everything inside me stops for a moment—breath, heartbeat, cottage pie and best bitter swirling through my intestines . . . everything comes to a halt. I know I ought to respond to this, but I don't. I wait.

'You could come back home with me,' Julie tells me softly.

I feel this upsurge of emotion and find myself, instinctively, moving my body away from her to save the embarrassment of her noticing the physical effect she's having on me. I feel fantastically high and yet, at the same time, there's something else I hadn't bargained for. Something that holds me back. I feel an awareness that, in spite of the fact that I've been waiting for this to happen for longer than I can remember, I'm afraid. I hate to have to admit this, but it's true—I actually feel quite shy.

'You could stay the night if you wanted to . . .'

I don't know where to put myself. I'm aware of the fact that Mike and Ralph have stopped their conversation and it seems as if they're listening, waiting to hear how I'm going to react. I feel embarrassed. I want to say yes—and yet I can't. My mum and dad will be waiting up for me—they'll get the police out searching, if I haven't arrived home by twelve o'clock—I can't just phone them up and tell them I'm sleeping with an unknown girl instead.

I stare down at my beer. I wish Mike and Ralph would start talking again, but they don't. The silence continues and I feel as though everyone's ears are tuned in, waiting to hear what I'm going to say. 'I'd like to come . . .' I mutter, still gazing downwards. I can't even bring myself to meet her eyes.

'Sorry . . .' says Julie, leaning across towards me. 'What did you say?'

I feel mortified. I have to say it again but louder. 'I'm sorry . . .' I start off, forcing myself to look up at her at last. I try to tell her with my eyes how much I want to spend the night with her. The words lie strangled in my throat. 'I've got to go home,' I manage to stammer. My chest feels tight with the frustration building up inside me. I don't want anyone to see the pain erupting in my face.

I take Julie's hand between both of mine and squeeze it hard. Then I stand up. I wish I could take Julie with me. I wish, at least, that I could thank her, that I could say to her: *Julie, I think you're fantastic. More than anything else I want to spend the night with you . . .* But no. The words clog up together like a wire hedgehog wrapped around my tongue.

I smile shyly. 'Thanks,' I tell her. 'Some other time . . .'

Julie nods and smiles back at me. 'Cheers, Chris,' she says.

'Cheers.'

I let go of Julie's hand and walk away, leaving my glass of beer half-empty on the table.

I walk outside, hating myself, into the silent street. I feel like searching for a tiny alleyway where I can sit down in a corner and hide, curled up like a squirrel with my arms wrapped round my knees.

I have to catch the bus. At first I just walk quickly, but then I speed up. I have to reach the bus-stop on time. I start to run. I concentrate all my attention on stamping my feet down hard, emptying my mind, pounding down the remorse and disappointment that have been seething away inside me. My footsteps echo round the empty street as I force myself to run harder, straining all my muscles. It feels good somehow to push myself, to make myself suffer, causing the soles of my feet to ache and my chest to tighten as I try to catch my breath. The anger and frustration that have been bubbling away inside me come crashing down and start to seep into the silent surface of the street.

I reach the bus-stop, panting with exhaustion.

I climb on board the bus and stagger to a seat down near the front. I want to sit alone.

My breath starts to come more easily as the bus sets off and I can sit back and relax. The rage I felt has gone and in its place there comes a strange and new sensation, something I hadn't expected. I think back to the way I felt when Julie invited me to spend the night with her and, even though I turned her down and made a mess of things, the image of her holding out her hand to me is something real and powerful and strong.

I know that what has happened is an opening, a crack of light inside the shell that's wrapped around me. Some day soon I have to break out. The shell is thin and brittle and it isn't made to last. It's made for breaking, forcing a way through. Inside the shell it's warm and damp, but damp with the stickiness of wings that are ready to be tested. The bones and muscle for the wings are waiting, and the strength in them is potent, wound up tight with tension. Some day soon I've got to break the shell and test the wings.

I have to learn to fly.

The light's showing between the curtains in the living-room as I walk up the drive. I wish they wouldn't wait up for me. I wish they'd go to bed and not worry what time I get back. I know they'll moan at me for staying out late; they usually go to bed at ten o'clock.

'Is that you, Christopher?' my father calls out as I slam the door behind me. Who does he think it is? Jack the Ripper? The rampaging werewolf of Hagg Farm Lane?

'Hello,' I call back from the hall as I start to sprint up the stairs to the bathroom.

'Where've you been till this time?' I can hear my mother's voice from the living-room. I wish I didn't have to talk to them. I don't know what they'll say if they notice that I smell of beer.

When I've finished at the toilet, I rinse my mouth around a couple of times with water before I go back downstairs.

When I walk into the living-room, they're sitting on the settee in silence. The television's off and my mother's wrapped up all her knitting. She's sitting with it on her knee, fastened up in the special drawstring bag in which she keeps her wool. They both look old and tired. I don't know what to say to them.

'Sorry I'm a bit late.' I try to sound normal and cheerful, and not breathe out too heavily. I don't want the room stinking with beer fumes. 'I missed the other bus.'

They just sit there gazing at the emptiness between us. They didn't want me to go to the meeting or the film, but there was nothing they could do to stop me. They didn't really try. There's nothing they can do to stop me going out late or having a drink before I come back home. They know I'm growing up and leaving them behind.

'It's very late,' my father says.

'The meeting didn't finish till late.'

'Your mother's been worrying about you. We didn't know where you were.'

I start to feel indignant. I was invited to spend the night with Julie and I turned it down so I could come back home and stop them worrying about me. They could at least be grateful. 'I told you where I was going,' I say to them, and my voice is hard and angry.

'You didn't tell us that you wouldn't be home until half past eleven.'

I look at my watch. It's eleven twenty now and I've been home nearly ten minutes. 'I wasn't back at *half past eleven*,' I snarl at them. I don't want to hurt them, but I can't stop myself from being angry. 'I was in the house by ten past eleven. I didn't ask you to wait up for me . . .'

'We just don't want you to get in any trouble, Christopher,' my dad explains, trying to keep calm. I hate the way he calls me Christopher.

'Meeting up with all these radicals . . . we don't want you to get involved.'

I take a deep breath, then I remember to hold it just in time to prevent the fumes from sailing over the top of the settee. 'It doesn't matter what you want,' I tell them, and my voice is harsh and cruel. I could have gone to bed with Julie. I could have stayed out all night. Other kids have freedom and independence; they don't have morons like this waiting up to see what time they come back home at night. It's all their fault that I'm nearly ready to start shaving and I haven't screwed a girl yet.

'I'm old enough to make my own decisions,' I tell them. 'If I want to get involved, I will. I'm involved already because I care about what's happening in the world. I don't just want to spend my life sitting at home watching the television every night . . .'

'We're not asking you to . . .' my father starts to interrupt, but I don't want to hear him. I feel angry and frustrated. I don't want to hear their point of view. I shake my head at my father and narrow my eyes with scorn. 'Leave me alone,' I tell him slowly and I no longer try to keep the hatred from my voice. 'Just leave me alone.'

I slam the door behind me and walk upstairs. I climb

into my cold and empty bed and cling on tightly to the pillow, almost crying with frustration.

The pillow is no substitute but, in the end, it has to take what I so much wanted to give Julie. I fall asleep, spent and hollow.

5

ARE YOU GETTING ENOUGH?
new clothes to be able
to give away some
of your old ones?

LOOK INSIDE YOUR DRAWERS
and try to find something
to donate to the
Ryecroft Peace Group
Jumble Sale

For further info: see Chris Fieldsend

That's the little card I pin on the notice board in the form room. The wording's stupid, but you have to write something like that to make the kids in our class take notice.

Of course, the only person who brings me anything at all

is Helen Wheatley. She rushes across at break the next day with a carrier-bag full of Pony Club annuals and two half-empty bottles of skunk juice.

'I saw your notice.' She giggles like a gas-filled gibbon. 'I've brought you some things for the jumble sale.'

She insists on taking every item out of the plastic bag, so I can say what a clever girl she is and how nice the pony annuals are and how thrilled somebody will be to buy a half-empty bottle of bargain-priced skunk juice. I wish she'd hurry up and go away.

'Where is the jumble sale?' she asks me.

Oh no! I don't want her turning up. If she insists on coming along, I'll have to stay at home. I tell her the name of the church, knowing full well that it won't mean anything to her. It's not exactly the poshest part of town, not quite Helen Wheatley land.

'Thanks a lot,' I say, scooping up the stuff, ramming it into the bag and revving off before she's got chance to ask me any more. There are at least eight hundred boys in our school. What's wrong with the other seven hundred and ninety-nine? It's nice to be good-looking, but only when it sets me up with girls I fancy—not when it gets Helen Wheatley sticking on to me like a Fuzzy Felt that's lost its box.

A couple of other kids ask me about the jumble sale. I explain to them about the peace group but, although they nod and say, 'Oh yeah,' and 'Great,' you can tell straightaway that they think it's something nice kids like them shouldn't get involved in.

It's like when I told Lee Furgusson on the bus about the film the other week. 'I went to see *The War Game* last night,' I mentioned after we'd nattered about the chess match and the previous night's homework and all that boring stuff.

'Is that a film?' he asked me.

'Yes.' What did he think it was? A flying ballet?

'Who was in it?'

There are a thousand and one questions you might reasonably ask of someone who's just been to see a film about the nuclear holocaust, but *who was in it* isn't one of them. I looked at Lee in despair. 'I don't know who was in it,' I told him. 'It's like a documentary. It's about nuclear war.'

Lee looked slightly more enthusiastic then and he started prattling on about some film he'd seen on TV about a nuclear war—one of those disaster movies that were all the rage five or six years ago.

I really felt fed up. It wasn't that I minded listening to Lee re-telling all the plot of this boring film in minute detail, though that was bad enough. It just felt so frustrating, wanting to share the way I felt with someone and not knowing anybody that I could talk about it with. I listened to Lee telling me how this multi-millionaire (whose name he couldn't remember) had kidnapped this film star (whose name he also couldn't remember) and had threatened to press the button that would blow up the world, if her boyfriend (whose name Lee could remember, but I can't) didn't do something completely boring and insignificant that isn't worth remembering anyway.

What happened was that I sat there feeling . . . I was going to say *lonely*, but that's not quite the word I want . . . feeling separate . . . sitting next to Lee Furgusson, smiling and nodding at him and feeling as though the two of us were about as close together as neighbouring galaxies.

Sometimes I get this awareness . . . I don't know what else to call it . . . an awareness of being alone. A feeling that I'm on my own, standing on the outside looking at people like a space-invader, an android . . . smiling and nodding at their futile conversations and their minds packed tight with trivia. Making all the right responses I've been programmed to produce and knowing that, however hard I try, I can never become quite like them; I'll always be apart.

That's one of the things I like so much about the peace group: a feeling that I'm with other people who think and see the same way that I do. People who care about what's happening in the world instead of just closing their eyes to all the things that seem too hard to cope with.

There might be nothing much we can actually do that will stop the world from being blown up. If it does happen one day, though, the tragedy will be that so many people realized it was on the cards and never did anything to try and stop it. I just want my name written down somewhere as one of the people who didn't go gently—as one of those who raged a bit to try and stop it happening.

This is what I'd like written on the plastic bag they wrap me up in:

HERE LIE THE MANGLED, BURNT-OUT,

RADIOACTIVE REMAINS OF

CHRIS FIELDSEND,

WHO DIDN'T TAKE IT LYING DOWN.

6

I arrive at the Revival Church fifteen minutes early and already there's a massive queue of people waiting to go in. There are harassed-looking mothers with pushchairs and stacks of little kids, climbing up and down the walls and leaping off the window-sills; there are old women with massive shopping bags and headscarves and a few old blokes who look like tramps. You don't see people like that on Hagg Farm Lane.

I walk to the front and push my way inside. As soon as I walk in, I'm met by a suffocating pong of musty woodwork and old clothes. I can see why they call it the Revival Church—anyone would need reviving after they'd spent an hour in here. People are dashing up and down with armfuls of old pyjama bottoms, women's corsets and jumpers that look like the kind of thing the Ancient Britons used to wear. I notice Mrs Hardacre, our R.E. teacher from school, setting out some cups and saucers on a table at the other side of the room. She wears a peace badge at school, but I didn't know she got involved with things like this. I give her a smile and wave before I tip up my carrier-bag on the nearest trestle table and have a word with Miss Meadows, who's busy sorting out the kind of old felt hats that Worzel Gummidge wouldn't be seen alive in. 'Where shall I put this stuff?' I ask her.

'Let's have a look.' She arranges Helen Wheatley's annuals on what she calls the 'fancy goods stall'. You wouldn't find goods less fancy in a dustbin. Then she catches sight of the two hand-knitted sweaters that I've hidden under all the other rubbish. 'Just look at this!' she exclaims, holding up a little number in gore-red clotted mohair. 'Surely somebody's not giving *this* to the jumble sale! There's nothing wrong with it.'

Nothing wrong with it! The design on the jumper was supposed to be a soccer player heading the ball—*just right for a boy*, it said on the pattern. It never occurs to the people who design knitting patterns that there are some boys who despise football. It didn't come out right, anyway. The player's head and the football were exactly the same size and colour so it looked as though, after a pretty violent match, a footballer's head was whizzing across the pitch. My mother had just knitted up to the footballer's armpits, when my dad tore off the bottom of the pattern for some paper to light his pipe with, so the rest of the front had to be knitted just plain. Can you imagine walking around in a jumper with half a headless footballer on the front aiming his opponent's skull into the goal?

'Somebody's put hours of loving work into knitting it,' Miss Meadows prattles on.

I start to creep away from her, round the corner to the shoe stall, where I notice that there's no one helping. I try to sort out some of the odd shoes into pairs.

'And just look at this lovely perfume somebody's brought!'

I wince and concentrate on finding partners to a pixie's ballet shoe and a bright pink furry slipper with a dead racoon's head on the front. Suddenly, there's a stampede —a raging mob sweeps through the hall like a tidal wave of triceratops and I realize that the jumble sale has started. When the crowd arrives at the shoe stall, I have to lean with all my weight against the wall. Most of the shoes I've managed to pair up neatly at the front of the stall go flying in the air or sliding on to the floor. I dive underneath the stall to rescue some of them, but the weight of the crowd pushes the table back against the wall, trapping me underneath.

As I scoop up armfuls of shoes, I spot the sleeve of a leather jacket sticking out beneath a pile of musty suits and overalls on the next stall. I yank it out and put it to one side. I can try it on later when the crowd's eased off. By now, there's about fifty pairs of arms waving at me with shoes or money or both. 'How much are these?' a woman asks me about a pair of high-heeled boots.

I know that boots can cost at least thirty to fifty pounds in the shops, so I ask her for a pound. I think that seems quite reasonable.

The woman couldn't look more horrified if I'd asked her to pay for them in alligator's eyeballs. '*What?*' She starts swearing and cursing out loud, using words you've probably never heard outside a football ground. 'A pound he asked me!' she tells the people round the stall. 'A pound for a pair of old boots!'

'It's a jumble sale, lad,' an old bloke tells me. 'You're not at Sotheby's now.'

I grin at him. 'Fifty p.?' I ask the woman.

'*Fifty pence!*'

'Thirty?'

'I'll give you fifteen,' she tells me, shoving the money into my outstretched hand and disappearing with the boots into the crowd.

After that I start to charge ten pence for all the ordinary shoes and fifteen for anything special. I haven't decided yet what to charge for all the odd ones. I'm still waiting for a one-legged pixie to come pirouetting through the Revival Hall looking for a new ballet pump, or for a decapitated racoon to wander in. I sell dozens of pairs of shoes and my saucer on the table starts to get piled up with money.

When the crowd's eased off, Mrs Hardacre comes across and brings me a cup of milky tea and a biscuit. She chats to me about the jumble sale and the peace group. I'm glad she doesn't say anything about school. I couldn't stand meeting a teacher outside school, if she just asked me idiotic questions about how much homework I'd got and how many exams I'm supposed to be taking.

Whilst I'm drinking my tea, I notice a girl strolling round, glancing at the stalls. There are quite a few kids of my own age buying some of the really way-out stuff we've got—some of the clothes we're selling are so way-out, they're just coming back into fashion—but this girl doesn't look the type somehow to buy her clothes at a jumble sale. Her clothes are casual, but they look expensive.

After a while, she walks over to my shoe stall and smiles at me. 'I haven't seen you before,' she tells me. 'Are you a member of the peace group?' Her voice is sort of smooth and cultured.

'Yes,' I tell her. 'I've not been a member for very long, though.' That seems a bit of an overstatement, considering that I've only been to one proper meeting so far.

I tell her about the last meeting that I went to. She asks me when the next one is and reaches into her leather shoulder-bag to take out her diary and make a note of the date.

Her bag isn't crammed with rubbish the way that most girls' are. She has a proper wallet in there and a cheque book and a key ring. As she takes out her diary, I notice that inside the front cover is a transparent little wallet with an account card in for D.T. Farmers—that's the poshest department store in town. This girl must be loaded. I notice the name on the account card: Sarah Barnforth. I think I've heard the name before somewhere, but I can't think where.

She only looks about the same age as me, but she seems very sure of herself; I can tell that straightaway. She's not at all nervous about walking across and starting up a conversation with somebody she doesn't know.

'We're planning a demonstration and rally soon,' I tell her.

'Yes, I've heard about that.' She nods and looks straight at me. She has long brown hair that looks as if it's been cut that way, if you know what I mean—it doesn't just look overgrown. She's wearing perfume that smells very subtle and expensive. She's also very nice-looking.

'Is there anywhere here that I can buy a new badge?'

I haven't seen any badges on sale, but I want to try and sound helpful. I ask Mrs Hardacre who's bustling past, collecting dirty cups and saucers.

'Stewart was going to have a stall for literature and badges,' she tells me. 'I can't understand why he hasn't turned up.'

'Sorry,' I say to Sarah. 'You'll be able to buy a badge if you come to the next meeting, though.'

'I'll leave it till then, then.'

Sarah looks down at the piles of odd shoes still lying on the stall, then grins at me and shakes her head. 'It's a pity there aren't more one-legged ballet dancers in the peace group,' she remarks. 'They'd be set up for life here!'

I grin back at her, pleased to have met someone who thinks on the same range of kilohertz as myself. 'Well, if you meet any,' I say, 'you can tell them where to come and buy their shoes. We've got plenty left over.'

'Right. I will do.'

She smiles at me again and turns to go. 'I'll probably see you at the next meeting, then,' she tells me.

I hope so. This girl is quite fantastic. 'I'll look forward to seeing you,' I tell her. Very polite, but that seems to be her style.

'Bye.'

'Bye.'

I can't help myself from gazing after her as she walks out of the door.

7

When there's only a few more people left, wandering round the stalls, I decide to try on the leather jacket. I take off my Co-op special anorak and lay it down whilst I slide my arms inside the worn and creased black leather. It feels beautiful. The jacket is smooth and comfortable and it fits as though it's been made for me. I fasten the heavy metal zip. The jacket reaches to just above my hips.

Right at the other side of the room is an old cracked mirror hanging on the wall. I squeeze my way behind Mrs Hardacre and Miss Meadows who are engaged in a conversation and gaze at myself in the mirror. Great. I try opening the zip to halfway down my shirt and wearing the jacket with the collar standing up. That's even better.

Then I catch a few words of the conversation that the two women are having behind me. They're talking about somebody who's had an accident and has been taken to hospital. 'What's the matter?' I ask Mrs Hardacre.

'It's Stewart,' she tells me. 'He's been hurt in a car crash.'

'Stewart? The one who chairs the meetings?'

Mrs Hardacre nods.

'What happened?' I don't know Stewart all that well, but I feel quite upset to hear he's had an accident.

'He went out to pick up some leaflets and things with Wayne after lunch,' Mrs Hardacre tells me. 'They were just coming back through town. Nobody knows how it happened.'

I really feel sorry. I hope he isn't going to die or anything. 'What about Wayne?' I ask her.

'I don't know,' she tells me. 'But they're keeping them both in hospital. I think they've both been badly hurt.'

'Oh dear. How did you get to know?' I ask.

'Well, I phoned up Stewart's number to see what arrangements he'd made for taking away all the jumble we'd got left,' Mrs Hardacre explains. 'His girlfriend had just arrived back from the hospital.'

'I know we shouldn't think about things like this,' Miss Meadows says, 'but if it's anything serious, it means we'll have that other horrible man chairing all the meetings.'

'Who do you mean?' I ask her.

'Ralph somebody-or-other. He wanted to be the Chairman and, when he was outvoted, somebody suggested that we make him Vice-Chairman instead. We never thought he might finish up having to take the meetings.'

'Let's hope Stewart soon gets better,' says Mrs Hardacre. 'Nobody'll come to the meetings any more, if he doesn't.'

I go back to the shoe stall and add up the money that I've taken. It comes to £9.65½p, a Yugoslav dinar, a few pesetas and a blob of old chewing-gum. The takings from other stalls have been added up as well and altogether they come to £94. That's quite amazing. I start to help clear up the stuff that's left, cramming the old clothes and shoes into huge black plastic bags.

Suddenly, I remember the Co-op anorak. I turn around to the stall next to the shoes where I put it down. The stall hasn't been cleared up yet, but I can't find the anorak anywhere. 'Has anybody seen my coat?' I call out. 'I left it over here.'

Everybody comes and searches round. 'What's it like?' they ask me.

'Navy blue.'

'Have you seen it, Harry?' Mrs Hardacre asks the man who's been serving on the stall.

'I sold a nice coat about five minutes ago,' he tells me. 'It didn't have a red quilted lining, did it? And a sort of pointed hood with fur round it?'

I nod. That's the one.

'I asked for thirty p. for it, with it being in such good condition. I'm sorry,' he says to me. 'Was it yours?'

Everybody looks apologetic. They seem surprised when they turn and look at me and there's a great big grin spread right across my face.

I'm hoping that my mum won't notice about the anorak. If she doesn't see me wearing it for a month or two, she might forget I ever had one. My mother has a memory like an earwig with concussion.

I walk inside the kitchen with the leather jacket slung nonchalantly over my shoulder. 'Hello.' I greet my mother, tying my face in knots to give her a normal, there-isn't-anything-the-matter sort of grin.

My mother looks up from arranging the Saturday salad on her Spring Sonata china. I call it Spring Snot. It's just that same pukish shade of yellowy-green you see trickling out of little kids' noses in early March.

'Where's your coat, Christopher?' she asks me straight-away.

I sometimes think I could drive a herd of stampeding aardvarks through the kitchen and she wouldn't notice —but give her something completely superficial and irrelevant to think about and she polishes up her eyeballs like searchlights on the top of Colditz look-out posts.

All I can do is tell her the truth; she might even see the funny side of it.

'It got sold at the jumble sale,' I tell her, still clutching on to the casual grin. 'By mistake.'

My mother drops a bunch of spring onions into the Spring Snot sugar bowl and gawps at me in horror. 'It was nearly brand new!' she exclaims. If my mother's paid for something in the last decade, she calls it *new*. If it's within the last two years, she calls it *brand new*. My father has a sludge-brown suit in a kind of werewolf-tooth pattern that I think he bought ready for the Norman Conquest and he still calls it his new suit. I'll leave it up to you to guess how long he's had his old one.

'I don't know how I can get you another one,' she moans, picking out the spring onions and wiping them with the dish-cloth.

Good. I don't want a new anorak. Ever.

'Couldn't they find anything better to let you come home in than that old rag?' she says, gaping at my fantastic new jacket as if it's something she's found on the wrong end of a lavatory brush.

I don't say anything. I stand watching her arrange the salad: one lettuce leaf each, two spring onions, half a tomato, a slice of pink pressed ham and a third of a hard-boiled egg. Not only have we had salad every Saturday since I grew out of Farley's Rusks, but every salad has had exactly the same ingredients. Not only that, but all the ingredients have to be placed in exactly the same position on your plate. The lettuce leaf sits on the top lefthand corner, sort of up near Inverness and, if it's a big leaf, it sails out into the Irish Sea; the pink pressed ham goes on the right, between Edinburgh and Bridlington; the egg sits on the top of London and the onions roll across the south coast looking like long green drainpipes lying between the red tomato halves.

Why do we have to have everything just the same? Why can't Cleethorpes be under a lettuce leaf? Why can't Manchester be covered in coleslaw or salami? Or egg foo yung? Why can't the whole of the British Isles be flooded out with fried rice, king prawns and sweet and sour sauce?

I sit down at the table and start to eat my salad.

8

On Monday afternoons we have cross country. Lee Furgusson, who's not exactly slimline, waddles round the course, puffing and panting like a piglet in a sauna bath. He'll do anything to get out of it.

Today, feigning terminal appendicitis, Lee manages to get sent home straight after lunch. I finish up taking his place in the chess team and I don't have an easy match. I win, but only after moving one of my pawns down to the bottom and swapping it for a queen. I feel a bit disgusted with myself. I don't have any obvious distractions this week, like I'm not preoccupied with playing footsie underneath the table or anything (and if you could see Gary Shepherd, the seven-foot iguanodon that I'm playing against, you'd understand why), but my mind still isn't on the game. I'm going to the peace group again tonight and the chances are that Julie will be there and the thought of that does things to my metabolism that I never thought were possible. I know she isn't going to chat me up and ask me to come home with her again; I know that because I've been saying it to myself over and over again all week. I just wish that certain parts of my body that I'm too polite to mention would hurry up and get the message.

Anyway, my chess game carries on so late that I miss the normal bus back home and have to stand around for twenty minutes in the cold and drizzle, waiting for the next one. *Come back, Helen Wheatley*, I find myself humming, *all is forgiven*. On evenings like this, I might just be able to force myself to step inside her daddy's Rover without feeling like a trapped hyena lured inside a mobile cage.

It's late when I get home. I eat my cottage pie with damp clothes steaming off me. Then I dash upstairs and have a shower, and I enjoy the sensation of hot water bouncing off my skin. I feel even better when I've changed into my jeans and leather jacket. I smile at my reflection in the mirror.

When I finally get myself to Ryecroft, the meeting is already under way. Ralph's right at the bottom end of the room, acting as the Chairman, and all the rest of the D.A.M.N. group, including Julie, are down there with him. Julie looks up briefly as I walk into the room and she kind of nods and half-smiles at me. I perch on a stool near the door.

I notice Sarah, the girl who came to the jumble sale, sitting at the other side of the room. She's nicer looking than Julie but in a different sort of way, kind of smooth and very pretty. She's wearing a round-necked sweater in that soft material that makes you feel as if you'd like to warm your hands on it. When Sarah looks at me, I smile at her, then try to concentrate on Ralph, who's droning on about Stewart being in hospital. To listen to him talk, you'd think the two of them were best mates. He's suggesting that the group should have a collection for Stewart and buy something to take to him in hospital. Everybody starts dipping in their pockets and taking out loose cash, and Harry, the bloke who sold my coat, offers his cap to collect the money in.

Whilst Harry's cap circulates round the room, Ralph starts to speak about the rally. Everything's well organized—it's just a question of going through all the last-minute arrangements, checking up on who's doing what. The Action Group have got themselves down as stewards. People exchange a few glances, but, since no one else has volunteered, there doesn't seem any reason to object. The march won't be just people from our town; there are about fifteen coaches coming, bringing people from different places round about. It all sounds really good.

Ralph goes through the list of speakers. 'There's one problem that's arisen,' he explains, downing his pint of bitter and lighting up a cigarette. 'Wayne, as you know, was going to speak briefly at the rally about the importance of getting more young people involved in the movement. He's not been as badly hurt as Stewart, but he's unlikely to be out of hospital for quite a while. What I'm suggesting is that we ask another young person to speak instead of him.' He pauses, taking a drag on his cigarette. 'The person I'd like to nominate,' he says, 'is Chris Fieldsend.'

My eyeballs swizzle back into their sockets after standing out and ogling Sarah's cuddly jumper. *Me, make a speech at the rally?* I grow about fifteen centimetres in my seat and find my face beginning to glow. Then I stop myself in time. It would be better to give the impression that I make a rousing speech in front of thousands every morning after downing my Sugar Puffs.

Most people are looking at each other clueless. They don't even know who I am.

'I'd like to second that,' Mrs Hardacre calls out. 'I teach Christopher in school and he's a very sensible young man. He speaks nice and clearly and, if he'd be willing to make a speech at the rally, I think he'd be very good.'

'What about it, Chris?' Ralph asks.

Just before I say yes, I'm aware of something flickering in the back of my mind: a red light. A tiny part of my brain that seems a bit more wide-awake than the rest, suddenly asks: why me?

I glance around the room at Ralph, Julie, Mike, Mrs Hardacre, who are all waiting for my reaction . . . I don't want to let them down. 'Yes.' I nod at Ralph. 'I'll do it.'

He smiles. 'Thanks, Chris,' he says. 'If you see me afterwards, I'll have a word with you about it.'

He goes on to talk about leaflet distribution and arrangements for hiring megaphones and who's going to make sandwiches for people at the Civic Hall, but I just sit there, glowing. All the other business of the meeting starts to fade into a distant blur as I see myself standing on the platform of the Civic Hall with the spotlights blazing and thousands of faces staring up at me. I hear them cheering me as I make a speech that brings tears to their eyes and has them on their feet, applauding. I haven't worked out the actual wording of the speech—at the moment it's nothing more than a jumble of phrases that I've picked up from Sixteen-Plus English Lit.: 'To die or not to die, that is the question . . .' And, 'I come to bury the Bomb, not praise it . . .' The audience love me. Their applause is still echoing inside my head, when I suddenly realize that the meeting has finished and people are standing up and starting to move away.

I look around for Julie. She's standing at the bottom end of the room with the other people in the Action Group. I start to make my way towards her. I don't know what I'm going to say to her, but I've got to keep cool and calm and friendly.

Before I've time to make my way across, Mrs Hardacre stands in front of me, blocking my way forward like an oversized police dog at a football match. 'I'm so glad that you agreed to speak at the rally, Christopher,' she tells me.

'Thanks,' I say, peering over her shoulder. I can just see Julie turning round and picking up her shirt.

'Well, I remembered how well you spoke when we had that debate last term in R.E. . . . now, what was it about?'

'I can't remember . . .' I spoke on the importance of sexual freedom in society, but that's not a subject that I want to think about right now.

Julie is making her way between the chairs. I send thought-waves across the room like lasers, willing her to turn and look at me. She glances in my direction, just long enough for me to raise my eyebrows. I don't have time to give her the sexy smile I've been rehearsing all week for her benefit, or even to mime if she'd like to come downstairs and have a drink. She just nods at me for a second, then disappears out of the door with Trevor. Damn.

'Was it about school dinners?' Mrs Hardacre asks me.

'What?' I turn and look at Mrs Hardacre as if it's the first time that I've seen her.

'Weren't you debating the case for charging an economical price for school dinners?' she asks me.

'No.' She's probably been confusing me with someone else all the time.

'Well, I'm sure you'll speak very well, anyway,' she tells me. 'I'll look forward to hearing you.'

I smile nicely at her. 'Thanks very much,' I say as I walk down to the other end of the room, where Ralph has a stall that's selling badges and literature. Also on sale are the badges that the Action Group wear and some books and pamphlets that have the same logo. Sarah has bought a couple of the peace group badges and now she's studying the books and leaflets. I'd like to get really close to her, taking long deep breaths of her perfume, but I manage to restrain myself and keep a respectable couple of centimetres away.

'Can we sell you a copy of *Action*?' Ralph asks her.

Sarah shakes her head. 'You know what I think about that,' she tells him. 'You won't get me to support a campaign I don't agree with.'

'If you don't buy the paper, then you're not even reading the arguments . . .'

'I've heard them all before,' Sarah tells him. 'All your group are doing is weakening the peace movement. You're getting bad publicity and losing us support.'

Ralph sighs and shakes his head. 'It's not publicity that matters,' he tells her. 'It's not publicity that'll stop the missiles—it's Direct Action. O.K., so we've had tens of thousands of people out on marches and demos, but what's that achieved? If a fraction of those people joined us in trying to smash down missile bases, then we could stand a chance of being successful. It's people like you and your father speaking out against us that weakens the campaign. Not us.' He picks up a copy of *Action* and offers it towards her. 'The least you could do is buy our paper and read through some of the arguments.'

Sarah shakes her head. 'I won't support a movement that believes in violence. I'm all in favour of Non-

Violent Direct Action, but there's no way you'll get me to support a group that throws petrol bombs and bricks at the police . . .'

'If they're standing in the way, then we've got to bloody well chuck things at them . . .'

Mike has come over to talk to Ralph as well. Sarah takes no notice of him but carries on her conversation with Ralph, speaking quietly but assured and very determined. She doesn't even look at Mike. He shifts impatiently from one foot to the other, angry at being ignored. His eyes travel up and down Sarah's body with all the subtlety of a hungry shark. I mentioned before that Sarah is very good-looking, but it seems a bit much to just stand eyeing her up as aggressively as that. I think any other girl would feel really embarrassed.

Mike turns to Ralph. 'I'll see you later,' he tells him. 'I'll get you a pint in down the road. O.K.?'

'I'll be along in five minutes.'

I don't want Ralph to go before I've had a word with him about the rally. 'About this speech . . .' I start off.

'O.K., Chris.' Ralph turns to Sarah. 'Can't we sell you anything else, then?' he asks her.

'No thanks. I've got everything.'

I wish I could think of things to talk to Sarah about, but I don't know enough about the peace movement to carry on the conversation she's been having with Ralph and I can't think what else to say to her.

Sarah turns round and smiles at me. 'Thanks for telling me about the meeting,' she says.

I inhale deeply on her perfume and force myself to look straight at her. Her eyes are deep hazel, I notice, and they wrinkle in the corners when she smiles.

'I'm pleased you could come to the meeting,' is all I can bring myself to say.

Sarah puts her wallet away inside her shoulder-bag. 'Yes,' she says. 'I should be able to get to all the meetings now I'm back at home.' She fastens her bag and turns to leave. 'I'll look forward to hearing you at the rally,' she tells me.

If Sarah wasn't so far out of my class, I could really bring myself to fancy her. I just grin at her like an imbecile. 'Thanks,' I say.

'Bye.' Her skirt brushes against my thigh as she walks away towards the door.

'Good-bye.'

'There isn't much to tell you, Chris,' says Ralph, picking up the leaflets from the table. 'Wayne's got a speech I can pass on to you. You won't need long to look through it. It's not difficult or anything.'

'O.K.' Actually, I would like plenty of time to look through what I'm reading. I've not had that much practice at public speaking. I could do with standing in front of my bedroom mirror, playing the speech over on my tape recorder, but I don't want Ralph to know that.

'One thing you've got to make sure of,' he tells me, 'is that you're right down at the front of the march. Just behind the banner, we've got the platform party—all the V.I.P.'s and everybody. You'll have to march with them.' He looks up at me. 'There'll be a seat reserved for you on the platform with the other speakers.'

'O.K.'

'And if you go backstage, you get tea and sandwiches and things while we're waiting for the hall to fill up. It'll take about half an hour.'

Very nice. I can just see myself hobnobbing and sharing a crab-paste sandwich with our local bishop and M.P. 'When do you think I'll get the speech?' I ask Ralph. I'm starting to worry now in case I have real problems reading it. My nerves'll probably be like wet blancmange.

'Well, I'll promise you one thing,' says Ralph. 'You'll get it some time before the rally. O.K.?'

I don't see why I shouldn't have the speech next week or even tomorrow, but I don't want to argue with him.

'O.K.' I tell him.

Downstairs the bar is just as crowded as it was last week, but I can't see Julie anywhere. The only people who've stayed behind to have a drink are Harry and Mrs Hardacre. Having a pint of beer in a pub with my middle-aged R.E. teacher would be a bit much, even if I wasn't under-age. I just wave and call good-night to them as I walk outside. I feel disappointed about Julie but, in a way, I was expecting it. I think about telling the kids at school that I'll be making a speech at the rally, just letting it drop casually into the conversation, as if I'm thinking nothing of it.

I hear the sound of applause again as I make my way towards the bus-stop.

9

The morning of the rally, I wake up with my guts tied up in knots and my stomach floating up and down my body like a sea-sick yo-yo.

I've got a placard that says, HELP THE GOVERNMENT TO SURVIVE—KNIT THEM A NUCLEAR FALL-OUT SHELTER, and I've got an extra-large peace badge and I've got gut-ache and the bog-runs and the only thing I haven't got is this bloody speech that I'm supposed to be reading in three and a half hours' time.

I just try not to think about it. I don't know Ralph's phone number, so I haven't been able to contact him and he *did* say he'd be sure to let me have the speech some time before the rally, so I suppose I'll have to trust him.

The only people going to town on the bus from our estate are kids from school, old-age pensioners and all those couples like my mother and father whose cars are so precious that they daren't take them into town in the Saturday traffic. My dad refuses to drive his car anywhere where there are lorries, buses, bikes or the possibility of kamikaze pedestrians bouncing off the bonnet and splattering bits of blood and fractured bones over his laminated windscreen, metallic paint and ancillary driving-lamps.

I clamber on the bus with my enormous placard and manage to dig a little old lady with it on her knee-cap. 'Just look what you're doing,' she grumbles, reaching down to rub her leg.

Unfortunately, the wood on the bottom of the placard hasn't been smoothed down and a splinter of it catches the thread of her thick elastic stockings. As I edge away from her, I feel something suddenly tugging me and I look down and see this enormous thread stretching out of the woman's leg and unravelling halfway down the bus. I try to break it, but the woman's stockings must be made of steel wool or fibreglass or something, because it just won't give at all. I sit down on the nearest seat, tugging gently on the thread as I move the placard round in front of me. The thread unravels a bit more and I turn to see it stretching behind me like a tightened fishing-line. I can see this woman having real problems getting off the bus: either dragging me along behind her like a landed perch, or somersaulting over the line of thread and landing on the laps of the people opposite, who are all gazing hypnotized out of the window like a shoal of sardines in a submarine.

I lift the thread and try to bite it, but it's like eating my way through reinforced steel cable, so I decide to melt it instead. I bought some cigarettes and matches today—I don't normally smoke, but I thought it might help to calm my nerves before the rally—so I light a match and hold it to the thread. The steel wool shrivels up and, as I turn around in a panic in case it works its way back like a fuse and sets the old woman's leg on fire, I come face to face with this gigantic bus conductor, who's glowering at me like King Kong in an all-in wrestling match. 'There's no smoking downstairs,' he growls.

'I'm not smoking,' I tell him, putting the matches back inside my pocket.

His enormous eyebrows knit together like a pair of mating yaks. 'I heard you light a match,' he snarls, sniffing like a tracker dog and peering underneath the seat to find the phantom, lighted fag.

'I suffer from pyromania,' I tell him, 'but I try to keep it under control.'

His eyes bulge forward in disbelief and he glowers as if he'd like to tear my flesh from me and eat it raw.

'I won't let it happen again,' I say apologetically.

He still doesn't look convinced. 'Have you paid your fare yet?' he growls.

As I reach into my pocket for some change, the placard seesaws and slaps the bloke sitting next to me on the knee. He bristles at me like a haughty hedgehog, as I take out my money and pay the fare.

The bus draws near to town and I see scores of people walking along to join the demonstration. My stomach lurches over as I think of them all sitting in front of me at the Civic Hall, waiting to hear my speech.

I get off the bus and walk towards the street where the demonstration's setting off. The crowd thickens, with people straddling across the road, starting to unfurl their banners and lifting placards in the air. As I turn the corner, I can hardly believe it when I see the massive queue stretching away as far as I can see. There are scores of banners already in the air and a sea of heads and shoulders filling the street. There's someone shouting instructions down a megaphone and a brass band taking out their instruments and starting to tune up. The atmosphere is really good. I've only ever seen demonstrations on the television before and I never realized that it made you feel warm and good and excited to take part in something with all these crowds of people.

I walk across to the front of the march to the enormous Ryecroft banner that's just behind the first brass band. Ralph is busy unloading piles of leaflets out of the back of a decrepit Mini-van that looks like one of the leftovers from a Demolition Derby. 'Have you got my speech?' I ask him.

'Hang on a minute.'

He passes piles of leaflets to people waiting round about. The leaflets have the D.A.M.N. logo printed on the top. I hope nobody minds. Then Ralph reaches into his pocket and hands me a couple of sheets of paper stapled together at the top. 'Here you are,' he tells me. 'Sorry I couldn't get it to you earlier.'

I start to glance at the speech.

'It's no use trying to read it now,' Ralph says. 'You'll have plenty of time at the Civic Hall. With this turn-out, we should be there about an hour before we get everybody inside.'

'O.K.' I fold up the paper and place it carefully in the inside pocket of my leather jacket.

Ralph thrusts a megaphone into my hand. 'Will you just walk down, Chris,' he asks me, 'and tell people to line up on one side of the road. The police won't let us set off until we're better organized.'

'O.K.' I take the megaphone and give a practice cough down through the speaker. It doesn't sound any louder than my normal voice.

'It works better if you switch it on,' explains Ralph, clicking the little switch I hadn't noticed.

'Oh.'

I've never spoken to anybody through a loudspeaker and I feel scared of hearing the sound of my voice booming over the crowds.

'Tell them we should be ready to set off in five minutes,' Ralph tells me.

'All right.' I set off down the street.

'The march will be setting off in five minutes,' I squeak down the megaphone. My voice sounds like that of a mouse that's just been stepped on. I clear my throat and try again. 'Keep to one side of the road, please.' I speak slowly and clearly this time, as if I'm used to giving people orders. Everyone starts to move back, lining up ready to start the march. I begin to feel more confident. 'We should be setting off in about five minutes,' I tell the crowd. I feel proud to think I'm one of the people who are helping to organize the demo, as I walk calmly up and down the middle of the street with the megaphone, shepherding everybody into place.

The stream of bodies, banners and placards goes on and on. The most colourful banners are the ones from different trade unions with their embroidered crests and illustrations. There are hundreds of people with home-made placards like mine—just pieces of hardboard and a stick with slogans that they've painted on themselves. Right towards the back of the march, I can see an open lorry with a rock group pounding away.

As I walk back towards the beginning of the march, I hear the sound of chanting. Things are getting really lively. Mike is walking down towards me with a megaphone in his hand, shouting slogans for the crowd to take up and repeat.

'One . . . two . . . three . . . four . . .' Mike's voice radiates strong and clear over the top of the placards and the banners.

'We don't want a nuclear war!'

'Louder. Come on, let's have it . . . One . . . two . . . three . . . four . . .'

The sound increases and I find myself tingling with goose pimples as I sense the latent power of all these hundreds of people . . .

'Come on, Chris,' Mike calls as he draws alongside me. 'Help us out!'

It was easy enough asking people to keep to the side of the road, but rousing them up with slogans is something else; I'm not sure if I can handle it. I'd feel such a fool if I shouted something and nobody answered.

I swallow hard, take a deep breath and yell into the megaphone, the same way Mike did: 'One . . . two . . . three . . . four . . .'

The crowd answers back: 'We don't want a nuclear war!'

This is really good. 'Five . . . six . . . seven . . . eight . . .'

The volume of the chanting voices spurs me with enthusiasm. I start again, my voice quivering slightly with emotion: 'One . . . two . . . three . . . four . . .'

The answering sound is powerful and strong, feeding me with confidence. There's nothing I can't do. I start to lose my nervousness and copy Mike, repeating other slogans down the megaphone:

'Missiles . . .'

'Out!'

'Missiles . . .'

'Out!'

'Missiles . . .'

'Out! . . . Out! . . . Out!'

The first part of the march has started to move off and, with a tremendous cheer, the people round about me started to walk forward. In front of us we can hear the sound of the brass band playing 'Jerusalem'. Passers-by are gathered thinly at the side of the road, staring at us.

As I reach the front of the march, I notice some of the kids from school. I'm surprised that any of them have turned out. I can see Lee Furgusson and, believe it or not, Helen Wheatley, complete with her father. I'm quite pleased when Helen notices me. Seeing me walking down the street with my megaphone ought to make it clear to her that she's hardly in my class.

I wave to Julie who's holding up the banner for the Action Group. I want Julie to notice me as well; I think she'll be impressed. I feel good when she smiles and waves back at me, but I'm feeling so high already that the extra boost to my hormones is something I can ride.

Right at the front of the march is Sarah, walking arm-in-arm with a strange-looking bloke, who, I assume, must be her father. He's about fifty years old with long, grey curly hair and a suit and tie. If he isn't her father, then she must have a very strange taste in boyfriends.

'Hello.' Sarah beckons me over when she sees me. 'May I introduce you to my father?' she asks me. 'You'll be together on the platform.' I can just make out what she's saying over the sound of the brass band. 'This is Chris Fieldsend,' she tells him. 'Chris, this is my father, Bevan Barnforth.'

He holds out his hand for me to shake, which is a bit awkward with the megaphone and the placard, but I manage it somehow. 'Pleased to meet you,' I tell him.

'How do you do,' he says to me.

So that explains where I've heard Sarah's name before and why she has her own cheque book, key ring and credit card. She's the daughter of our local M.P.

The crowd behind us has quietened down, so I decide to move out and do my routine again with the megaphone. We're nearing the centre of town now and people are lining the sides of the street, staring at us and holding up little children so they can get a better view. I had thought I might feel nervous about walking down the centre of the town with so many people looking at us, but I don't. I just feel great. We turn the corner and wheel round into the High Street where the pavements are already thick with Saturday shoppers. I hold the megaphone steady and send my voice echoing across the crowds and shops and lines of waiting traffic: 'Missiles . . .'

'Out!'

'Missiles . . .'

'Out!'

'Missiles . . .'

'Out! . . . Out! . . . OUT!'

'Come on, louder! Let's hear it . . .!'

For the first time in my life, I share the power of a mass of people, all with one voice, one aim, one intention. It had never occurred to me before that the handful of supporters helping at the jumble sale, or the audience sitting horror-stricken at *The War Game* could actually do anything to make the government change their minds. What I realize now is that the peace movement is more than that—it's people working together up and down the country, building up massive demonstrations to show that we won't sit back and allow ourselves to be wiped out just because some government thinks it's good for us. We're going to fight to stay alive. We're going to fight and rage and scream and cry out, and I think again about the poem by Dylan Thomas:

> 'Do not go gentle into that good night . . .
> Rage, rage against the dying of the light.'

And I know that there are people who are not going gently but are bent on rage, and it does my heart good to be here with them.

10

The march terminates at the Civic Hall, which is a huge circular building in the town centre where I've been a few times to hear different rock groups play. We walk inside the entrance hall and stand up the banners and placards, then turn down the corridor which leads backstage. The doors to the auditorium are standing open and, as I walk past, I can see the rows of empty folded seats all in dark red upholstery. I pause for a second or two at the door nearest to the stage and peer inside. The atmosphere is very still and quiet and there's a smell of polish. Everything is waiting, ready. I look upwards at the huge, domed ceiling with carvings round the edges and enormous lights hanging down like chandeliers and I start to feel small and nervous. The only people I've seen appearing on this stage are famous international rock stars and it's not easy to imagine myself running up the steps in the middle of the platform and grabbing hold of the microphone, full of confidence the way they do.

Behind the stage is a kind of large waiting-room, in which there's a table covered in a clean white cloth with sandwiches and drinks and cakes spread out on it. I can't understand why I don't feel hungry. I'd normally have eaten my lunch an hour ago. I just take a tiny triangle of bread and nibble at the edges like a daddy-long-legs on a diet. Then I go to find the bog—the special 'performing artistes' bog for people who are waiting to go on stage.

Once inside, I lock the door, pull down the heavy wooden seat and sink on top of it. I could perch here for half an hour, thinking about all the famous pop stars who might have sat here on this self-same bog, shitting with the thought of the thousands of kids screaming for them to walk out on to the stage. But I don't. I get out my speech and start to read it.

At first my eyes won't focus on the words. The printed letters stare at me like advertising captions on a hoarding: words that have no meaning; words your eyes can look at whilst your mind is focusing on something else. And my mind is focusing on the way my guts are twisted together like overcooked spaghetti. My stomach is churning round and round like an automatic washing-machine on a heavy-soil programme. I've got to calm myself down.

I take the cigarettes and matches from my jacket pocket, light a fag and inhale deeply. It doesn't make me feel much better, but it's something else for my guts to think about. I start to read the speech again. I read the first two paragraphs.

When I've read the paragraphs, I stop. I place the

papers on my knee and I stare at the door in front of me. I know what's happened. I can see it all: why they've chosen me to read the speech; why I haven't seen it until now. Suddenly, the whole scenario is spread out in front of my eyes as clear and lucid as figures on a computer display screen. The Action Group have written a speech which puts over their ideas and theirs alone. They weren't allowed to have a speaker at the rally, so they've written the speech and chosen me to read it, and they've chosen me because they think I'm young and stupid and won't complain about getting the speech so late and won't dare tell them that it isn't what I want to say.

I inhale again on the cigarette and raise myself to lift up the seat, so I can flick the ash into the bog. I don't know what to do. I'm not thick. I do know what they're doing; I can see right through their plans and schemes and they don't con me as easily as that. I think about altering the speech. I start reading it through again from the beginning. I hunt in my pocket for a pencil, but I haven't brought one. There isn't time, anyway. It would take me nearly half an hour to go through, altering the wording, and it'll soon be time for the rally to begin. I start to panic.

I wish I had somebody to lean on. I wish I had a brother or a best mate or a girlfriend, somebody to share things with. But I haven't. The feeling that sweeps over me is the feeling that I've had so many times before—the realization that I'm on my own. I don't belong to D.A.M.N.; I don't belong at home; I feel as though I belong with the peace movement, but what I'm doing now is going to betray it.

I haven't got long to make my mind up. I take another puff on the cigarette and throw it into the bog, where it sizzles as it hits the water. Then, I think about Sarah, leaning on her father's arm, chatting with him and laughing. And I think about my own father, pottering in the garden, polishing the bird muck off the hats of his garden gnomes, a thousand worlds apart from me and as out of place at a peace rally as a zombie in a disco.

But the image of Sarah stays with me. Sarah seems intelligent and practical and she might be able to help me re-write the speech in the last few minutes before the rally starts; she might even be able to ask her dad to help. I open the door and walk outside to look for her.

Standing outside the Gents is Julie. 'I thought we'd lost you,' she gasps at me. She looks genuinely relieved to see that I haven't been drowned in the bog.

'I've been looking through the speech,' I tell her.

Julie puts her hand upon my shoulder. Her face is shining with excitement. 'It's fantastic, isn't it!' she says.

'Well, it's . . .'

She doesn't give me time to finish. 'I typed it out for you the other night after Ralph had written it. It's a lot better than that thing Wayne was going to read.'

'Well, it's . . .'

'You'll be brilliant,' she tells me, squeezing her hand upon my shoulder. I can't pretend she doesn't make me feel good.

'Will you put these out upstairs?' Ralph dashes across and thrusts a pile of *Reserved* notices into my hand. 'The hall's getting full and we've got to keep the bottom row of seats on the platform free for all this lot . . .' He waves his hand at the crowd of people in the room. 'Will you give him a hand, Julie?' he asks. 'We'll be starting soon.'

'O.K.' Julie takes half the notices from me. 'Come on,' she says, walking over towards the doorway that leads out on to the stage.

I press the sharp edge of the cardboard into my sweating

palm; the pain is good for my concentration. I follow Julie through the door and up the steps.

We emerge into a blaze of light and sound. The entire hall is packed with people. Everywhere I look there are faces, crammed together row upon row. There are banners and placards everywhere. The lights are strong and dazzling, and the whole huge auditorium is a sea of chanting, cheering voices . . .

'Missiles . . .'
'Out!'
'Missiles . . .'
'Out!'
'Missiles . . .'
'Out! . . . Out! . . . Out!!!'

The whole tumultuous noise of the great long march is concentrated together here in a deafening barrier of sound. I stand transfixed. The surging power of the crowd is something real and live and potent, pulsing out in waves around me with the force of an explosion. The wooden boards of the stage beneath my feet still send vibrations through my body seconds after the sound begins to fade away. I could never have even imagined an audience like this. I feel terrified. I stand motionless and stare, open-mouthed, at the scene before me, gazing uncomprehendingly at the unleashed powers of the crowd.

'Isn't it fantastic!' Julie says to me. I hear the words, but nothing else registers upon my consciousness except the crowd, the noise and terrible power of all those hundreds and thousands of people.

'Come on.' Julie touches my arm. 'We've got to put the cards out.'

We turn round and spread out the cards along the vacant seats behind us, politely moving people away from the places that have already been allocated. I try to stop my hand from shaking as I stand the white cards on the seats. Then a voice breaks out from the top of the row of seats behind the stage:

'One . . . two . . . three . . . four . . .'

'We don't want a nuclear war!' the crowd chants back.

The enthusiasm of the crowd is so intense that I feel as though it could shatter me. Part of me dissolves in awe. I feel in danger of melting with emotion. I take a deep breath and force myself to keep control. This is the chanting that I helped to start off in the street. It isn't something alien and foreign: it's a sharing of solidarity; an overspilling of enthusiasm.

I begin to feel an excitement. The elation of the crowd is what I feel myself. In spite of the awe and fear and the terrible sense of power, I feel an empathy towards them: they are speaking for me, giving voice to my thoughts, shouting the words I want to hear. Suddenly, I don't want to stand back and listen any longer; I want to be with them and to share with them.

I walk down to the centre of the platform and face them, small and lonely, dwarfed by the enormous ceiling, the huge dazzling lights and the great expanse of space in front of me. I stand in front of them and pause, and then I clench the fist of my left hand and, slowly and deliberately, raise my arm high up into the air. They cheer—a sudden, erupting, hurtling onslaught of sound. But they cheer. They're with me. The gesture speaks to them and they answer. I have become a part of them and they are part of me, and I want to go on sharing this emotion, this solidarity. I want to read the speech.

I turn and run back downstairs with Julie, both of us glowing with excitement. 'Have you heard them?' Julie yells at Ralph. 'Have you heard what's waiting for us out there?'

Julie's voice infects everyone else in the room, but I can't allow myself to be drawn in. I find a seat in a quiet corner of the room, light up another cigarette, then take out my speech and start to read it through. I read it slowly and carefully, not worrying what the speech says, but concentrating only on how I'm going to read it aloud . . . where I should pause, what words I should stress.

As soon as I've finished my cigarette, it's time to walk up on to the stage.

As we emerge on to the platform, the auditorium is in darkness; only the stage is lit. An enormous cheer breaks out as the Lord Mayor leads the platform party up the steps and we take our seats behind the wooden tables. I still feel absolutely terrified, but it's not the threatening kind of fear I had before. It's not a fear of danger. It's a feeling of excitement and elation where all my nerve-endings are souped-up, stretched out, tingling with intensity. I lay my speech down on the table in front of me, so no one will notice the way my hands are shaking.

The Lord Mayor stands in front of the microphone. He starts to speak, although the audience hasn't really quietened down. 'As Lord Mayor of this city,' he says, 'I would like to welcome all of you here today.'

A tremendous cheer breaks out again from the audience, taking ten or fifteen seconds to die down.

'I'm very pleased the weather has stayed fine . . .' the Lord Mayor carries on . . . 'although it did look a bit cloudy round about half past ten.'

Someone on the balcony starts to boo. I don't know why, but the booing is taken up all round the auditorium. Nobody is the least bit interested in the Lord Mayor's weather report. They'd rather take part and be doing something.

Another voice from the back of the hall starts up the chanting again, and the Lord Mayor has to stand and wait nearly half a minute before he can fumble through the next part of his speech.

I don't even listen to what he's saying. It's something completely boring and irrelevant that the crowd don't want to listen to, and they just make a meal out of cheering and booing and bursting into chants again every ten seconds or so. I don't hear any more of the words. I know it's my turn next and I sit at the table petrified, taking long, deep breaths and squeezing my hands together so that I don't have to look at how they're shaking. I just hope the crowd will calm down before I have to get up and speak.

The Lord Mayor seems to realize that his speech isn't going down too well and he quickly brings it to a close. 'And now I'd like to introduce you,' he says, 'to someone who represents the hundreds of young people who have recently joined our organization . . . Chris . . . er . . . er . . .' He holds up the little card on which he's written down his notes . . . 'Chris Feellend . . .'

More shouts and cheering. This is it. I stand up calmly and make my way across to the microphone. The chanting starts again as I walk across the stage:

'Missiles . . .'

'Out!'

'Missiles . . .'

'Out!'

'Missiles . . .'

'Out! . . . Out! . . . Out!!!'

I walk over to the centre of the platform and stand behind the microphone, waiting for the noise to quieten down. As the last of the chanting dies away, I raise my left clenched fist to the crowd and again there's the massive response that I had before. 'It's going to be O.K.,' I tell myself. 'They're with me.'

I hold up the printed speech in front of me and there's nothing I can do to stop my hand from shaking. I grip the paper tightly so that the words keep still enough for me to read them. I wait for the hall to become silent, take a long deep breath, then read out the words slowly and clearly.

'There are thousands of young people like me on our march today,' I start off, 'and these young people have a message that we want everyone across the length and breadth of the country to hear—we will not allow the government to base its new missiles anywhere in the country.' I pause.

For a second or two there's no response. There's a short delay between my speaking the words and them echoing out from the huge loudspeakers situated round the hall. I'm just about to start the next sentence, when I become aware of the sound of the audience clapping. The sound builds up swiftly into a huge crescendo of noise that echoes around the high, domed ceiling. The clapping erupts into cheers. The sound is behind me and in front of me and at the side of me, so that I stand on the platform surrounded by a huge, vibrating box of noise. My whole body tingles in response.

I wait until the sound dies down. 'Our demonstration today,' I continue, 'was a show of strength.' I don't wait for them to respond to this; I carry on. 'We have shown the press, we have shown the government and we have shown the rest of the population just how much support there is for our campaign.' More applause. I wait just a few seconds; that's all. I don't want them to lose the thread of what I'm saying.

'No government can afford to ignore the strength our movement has shown today.' I pause slightly, but only long enough to let the words sink in. 'The task that lies before us now is to use that strength in any way we can.' I let the volume of my voice increase to emphasize the words I'm saying. 'The people of this country do have the power to stop nuclear missiles being based here.' More applause, but still I carry on, forcing the audience to listen with the strength and power of my voice. 'We can sit down in front of tanks and lorries, we can break down police cordons . . . if the government insist on deploying nuclear missiles against the wishes of the people, then we must storm our way inside the bases and smash up everything that's there. Here in this hall we have the power . . .' I hold out my outstretched hand as if the whole strength of the movement could be clasped within my trembling fingers. 'We must not shrink back,' I let my voice rise in a crescendo, 'from using that power in any way we can to stop nuclear missiles ever being used.'

As I speak, I can sense the atmosphere rising in the hall and I find I have to keep pausing to give way to the tumultuous cheers and stamping from the crowd. I become aware that I am speaking for them, giving voice to their thoughts, saying the words they want to hear. The crowd are applauding me because I have become the thoughts they want to express. I am their voice, their purpose. When they clap me, they applaud themselves.

I carry on with the rest of the speech, no longer feeling nervous, but delighting in the control the words give me of the crowd. I speak slowly and calmly to make them listen and then I allow my voice to rise in great crescendos of emotion, easing back and giving time for them to clap and cheer. They don't want to sit back and listen; they want to take part in the speech, adding their own choruses and rhythm. I start to love the crowd.

As I reach the final paragraph of the speech, I force

myself to slow right down, packing the words with meaning. I have no more misgivings as to what the speech is about; I know what it's about and I support it. I have never supported anything as strongly in my life before as the purpose behind this speech.

'We must not become diverted . . .' I tell the crowd . . . 'by pacifist propaganda. We must not be afraid of using violence. When the future of mankind is at stake, there is nothing . . . absolutely nothing . . . that we can afford to let stand in our way.'

11

After the rally, a great crowd of us go to the pub across the road. The bar is tightly packed with people, thronging round and squeezing their way past each other. Everyone keeps coming up to me and telling me how fantastic my speech was. I feel great. I know I spoke well, but it doesn't do any harm to hear people tell me so. I accept a pint of beer and hand round the cigarettes I've brought.

Julie walks over and puts her arm around me. 'You were fantastic,' she says, smiling up at me. Her face is warm and full of admiration.

'Thanks.' I grin at her and put my arm around her waist and squeeze her. We stand there for a few seconds, hugging each other. There's no way I can feel shy or nervous now. Julie wants to be with me and to be seen with me, and knowing that makes me really sure of myself. I'm a star.

I take a long, cool drink of the beer which tastes a lot better today. I realize just how dry my throat has been.

Then, still with my arm around Julie's waist, I lean across so that my mouth is only a few centimetres from her ear. 'Shall we go back to your place, when we've had a drink?' I ask her.

I look at her straight between the eyes, smiling at her, making it hard for her to turn me down. She's not going to say no, anyway. Nobody could say no to me today. Julie grins at me and nods. I know she's pleased I've asked her.

'O.K.' she answers.

I give her another squeeze before turning round and listening to Mike, Trevor and Ralph, who are still talking about the rally. 'We took a gamble on you, Chris,' says Ralph, swilling back his beer. 'We never thought you'd be as good as that. You were *brilliant*!'

I light up a cigarette and try to give an *Oh, it was nothing* sort of look, but I don't suppose it comes out like that. I don't feel modest. Like I say, I feel like a star. I feel as though I could do anything. I know I've got to leave the pub soon, if I'm going to make it with Julie, but all this praise and admiration isn't easy to tear myself away from.

'That Barnforth bloke had it in for you, Chris,' says Mike.

That was the only thing that put me down: Sarah's father. At the end of his speech he went on about how a peace movement has to be peaceful. I can still remember what he said: 'We can sympathize,' he lilted in his tuneful Welsh voice, 'with the impatience of young people who want immediate results. But those of us who've campaigned before know that violence will only split the movement. If we advocate peace, then we must practise peace. If we believe that peace is the way forward for our country, then we must practise peace ourselves.'

He got plenty of applause as well and I couldn't help wondering, as I sat there listening, whether people had cheered me so much just because I was at the beginning of the rally when everyone was so enthusiastic. It's possible that his ideas might have had more support than mine. Even I could see the logic in them; they just didn't move me the way my own words moved me when I was speaking them aloud.

'It's that Sarah that we're going to have to watch,' says Mike. 'She's the one who'll come to the meetings and plug all that pacifist garbage . . .'

That was the one other thing that put me down: the look on Sarah's face when I left the microphone and went to sit back at the table. Everyone else was applauding—even the people on the platform were clapping me politely —but Sarah just sat there frozen. Our eyes met for a fraction of a second and the expression on her face was one of unmistakable disgust, forcing me to lower my eyes down to the ground. In my greatest moment of triumph, she managed to make me feel like a kid at school caught masturbating in the bog. I felt as though she'd seen straight through me, right to the watery milk inside. It was a look that could wither the shell off a coconut.

'I'm not bothered what Sarah thinks,' I answer, with just the right touch of disdain. 'Or her father . . .'

'Well, it was obvious what everybody thought . . .' says Ralph.

I'm not sure if it was obvious, but I smile and nod.

'Yeah.' Trevor grins as he swills down his pint of beer. 'It was Chris that got all the applause.'

After a few minutes, I squeeze my way to the bar to get some change for the contraceptive machine. I hope they've got one. I don't know what I'll do if they haven't. I notice a pile of neatly-wrapped sandwiches on the edge of the bar. I've heard of kids using cling-film when they're desperate, but I'm not sure it would work. It would take me ages to get the crumbs off it, not to mention the bits of pickle and tomato sauce. It's not exactly the romantic approach that I was thinking of. I pick up the change and walk inside the Gents.

There's a machine on the wall. I could hug it. Just as I'm sorting out my change, though, the door opens and Trevor strides in. 'Hey up,' he mutters.

I move away from the machine, put the money in my pocket and start to use the urinal. Then another bloke walks in and starts to chat with Trevor. This could take all day. I don't know why I feel embarrassed about buying contraceptives with a couple of older blokes around, but I do. I spend three or four minutes washing my hands, putting on extra lashings of soap and scraping out my fingernails. I wish they would go. When they don't, I walk inside one of the cubicles, close the door and sit down on the bog. If I have to wait much longer, I'll find Julie's been chatted up by someone else and gone off home.

I breathe out a sigh of relief as I hear Trev and his mate closing the door behind them and I stagger out of the bog, the money poised ready in my fist. I'm terrified now that the wretched machine won't be working. I don't know how I could cope with the cling-film.

I walk across and drop in my money. It works! Easy. I take the packet and place it in the pocket of my jeans, then I walk back to the bar.

'Another pint, Chris?'

It's Trevor's turn to buy a round. I don't know how my other pint disappeared so quickly. I think I got thirstier than I realized with all that shouting and chanting. 'Thanks,' I tell him, 'although I will have to be going soon.' I know I mustn't put off going home with Julie. I've got to make tracks whilst I'm feeling high. I catch Julie's eye and wink at her, when I feel sure that no one else is watching. She grins at me.

I accept the beer from Trevor and start drinking it straight down. I'm feeling really good; I know everything's going to be O.K. Ralph walks across from the other side of the group and hands me a cigarette. 'I need to have a chat with you, Chris,' he says.

I accept the cigarette.

'About Sarah.'

'Mmmm . . .'

He lowers his voice and speaks to me more confidentially. 'That kid's a pain in the arse . . .'

I look up at him questioningly as I light the cigarette.

'She's forever standing up at meetings and moaning about us.' Ralph lights up his cigarette and throws the match towards an ashtray. 'She was away at one of those private boarding-schools before, so we only had her to put up with in the holidays. She's transferred to one of the local comprehensives now, so we'll have her all the bloody time.'

I take a drag of the cigarette. 'I thought she looked fairly harmless,' I tell him. 'She's only about my age.'

Ralph scoffs. 'That's the trouble,' he says. 'All the old biddies think she's great, because she looks nice and sweet and she's not much more than a kid. They go mad when Mike stands up and swears at her.'

I chuckle. I can just imagine Miss Meadows and Co. glaring at Mike in disgust.

'Have we got a meeting tomorrow, Ralph?' Mike asks.

'Hang on . . .' Ralph turns to me and lowers his voice again. 'I'll have a word with you some other time, then, Chris. I think you can help us out . . .'

'O.K.'

He turns back to speak to Mike and I finish off my beer. I'm not worried about Sarah at the moment. All I'm bothered about is Julie and setting off home with her. I give her a questioning look and she nods. I touch Ralph briefly on the shoulder. 'I'll have to be going,' I tell him.

'O.K., Chris.' He turns round and pats me on the back. 'Thanks again,' he says to me. 'You were really great.'

'Cheers, everybody.' I look around and grin at them all before I leave. It still feels good to know that they're all proud of me.

'See you, Chris.'

'Cheers, Chris.'

I walk out into the street with Julie.

We take the bus to Julie's house and it's crowded. Even though we go upstairs, we have to sit on separate seats. I sit next to an old lady in a fur hat, who's busy gazing out of the window, and I light up another cigarette. Actually, I don't mind sitting on my own because I'm not sure what to talk about with Julie. I feel as though it's kind of understood between us that we're going to go to bed together, but it doesn't seem right to talk about it—like asking her how she likes to do it and things. On the other hand, it seems a bit silly to just carry on a conversation about the rally and the overcrowding on the buses, as if having sex together couldn't be further from our minds.

Another reason why I'm pleased to sit on my own is that I need to work out how I'm going to handle the whole scene—like exactly what I'm going to do and say to her. The problem is that I've got such a hard on already and, if I think about it much more, I'll finish up shooting off all over the bus seat and probably the little old lady sitting next to me as well.

As if she could read my thoughts, the little old lady

turns round and glares at me. It's Miss Meadows. 'Oh, hello there!' Her face lights up when she sees me.

'Hello.' I try to sound enthusiastic.

She starts chatting to me about the rally. She hasn't heard any of the speeches because she's been so busy with the catering, serving cups of tea and making sandwiches. I smile and nod at her and try to work out whether I ought to spend time kissing Julie and whispering suggestions in her ear, or whether I ought to just dive straight into the bedroom, rip my clothes off and hope she does the same.

'I must have made fifty crab-paste sandwiches and three dozen cheese and tomato . . .'

The thought of all those mountains of sarnies turns my stomach over. 'Well, they were lovely sandwiches,' I tell her. 'You did a marvellous job.' I think I'll have to lead her into the bedroom straightaway. I don't think I can last out more than two or three minutes of anticipation.

'We had to send down to Sainsbury's for some extra cucumbers and tomatoes.'

I cross my legs and, when that doesn't work, I spread them apart and sit with my hands inside my jacket pockets, hoping Miss Meadows doesn't notice anything unusual. I don't want her to think it's her that's turned me on. I don't know if you've ever tried smoking a cigarette with both hands inside your pockets but, take it from me, it isn't easy.

'We got through six enormous cucumbers . . .'

I shuffle around and try not to think about the cucumbers. I wish my jeans weren't so tight. I'd have been better off in the baggy ones from the Co-op sale, after all.

I breathe out a sigh of relief as I see Julie walking down to get off the bus. I stand up awkwardly. 'I'll be seeing you,' I say to Miss Meadows. I turn and follow Julie down the stairs.

12

The terraced house where Julie lives has a tiny square of garden that grows nettles, grass and empty beer cans. My father thinks people should be taken to court for keeping their gardens like that.

She takes out her key and opens the back door, which leads straight into the kitchen. The room smells damp and greasy. There are dirty chip papers screwed-up on the floor and a pile of dishes in the sink with bits of curry sauce, cold chips and mushy peas still embedded in the grease. They look as if they've been there a day or two. On the plastic-topped table is a bowl of dried-up cornflakes, some empty beer cans, a filthy jam jar with the lid off, a couple of soggy tea bags and about fifty-seven cigarette ends. I think my mother would puke up if she had to have a meal here.

'Would you like some coffee?' Julie asks me.

I don't fancy anything to eat or drink and I haven't come here anyway to sit and chat and drink coffee. I don't want to get involved in a conversation that I find difficult to sidle out of.

'No thanks.' I take off my jacket and hang it up behind the door.

I mustn't wait too long. I've got to start making moves with Julie whilst I still feel as if I'm winning. I walk across and place my hands on Julie's shoulders and I smile at her. When she smiles back at me, I kiss her. It feels strange. Her lips are small and thin and childlike. Over Julie's shoulder I can see the plates of ancient curry sauce and chips piled up in the sink. I try not to look at them. I close my eyes and kiss her again, holding her around the waist.

I kiss her hair and then I move my lips gently down towards her ear. 'Where's the bedroom?' I mutter, trying to make the words sound soft and seductive. I don't know how I find the courage to say them, but I do.

Julie nods, then turns and leads me out of the kitchen and up the stairs. I follow just a little way behind, watching the way she moves her body when she walks and becoming aware, for the first time, that I'm feeling scared and nervous. I must have fantasized about this scene a hundred times or more, but I realize now that the real event won't be anything like a single one of the fantasies.

We walk inside the tiny bedroom and, even though it doesn't smell as bad as the kitchen, the mess is even worse. The bed is unmade and the floor is covered with piles of dirty clothes and screwed-up tissues. There's a chest-of-drawers littered nearly two-feet thick with leaflets, empty beer cans, more screwed-up tissues and a half-empty packet of Tampax.

'I'm sorry I haven't made the bed,' says Julie, straightening the sheet and picking up some stained brown pillows off the floor. I didn't know there were people who never used pillow-cases.

'That's O.K.,' I tell her. 'It'll only want making again afterwards.' I walk across and put my arm round her again and kiss her, only this time it isn't the kind of tentative experiment it was before. When she puts her arms around my neck and starts searching with her lips and tongue around my mouth, I find myself throbbing with sensations that are so intense they almost frighten me. All the books I've read about sex haven't prepared me in any way for coping with this sudden urgency—this drastic craving to simply let myself go. All the things I know I should be doing to make Julie feel turned on are simply words I've read on paper. The only thing I can concentrate on is what is going on inside me. And what's going on inside me now is pounding away so fast I feel as if I'm nearly ready to explode.

I disengage Julie's arm from my neck and push her gently away from me. 'Shall we get into bed?' I ask her.

Julie nods. If she'd said no, I think I'd have had to dive straight into the bathroom and shoot myself off in there. I've got to try and hold on the brakes. Pull in the reins on my stampeding blood vessels and hold myself back. I remove the packet of contraceptives from the pocket of my jeans and place them under the pillow. I hope I can wait long enough to put one on. Then I take off the rest of my clothes, looking at Julie all the time. I've never seen a girl undress. What I'd really like to do is just sit down on the edge of the bed and watch her, but I don't have time for that. My fingers fumble with my buttons and with the laces on my shoes, and I notice that I'm shaking. I wanted so much to be in control and I realize now that there is no way that can happen. What's in control is something that almost seems beyond myself, an unknown power moving me, carrying me forward—huge magnetic forces shifting me into position like a pawn pulsating on an electronic chess board. All that I can do is stand in front of the force and tremble, the way I stood on the stage at the Civic Hall, shaking at the unleashed power of the crowd.

Julie lies in bed waiting for me as I take off the rest of my clothes and fold them neatly on the floor. My mother always moans at me if I drop my clothes down without folding them and, although Mum can't see me now, I still go through the ritual. I climb into bed next to Julie and she turns and puts her arms around me. Her skin is soft and warm. All I can feel is pleasure.

I move my hands around her body, but it's not because I want to make her feel excited; what I really want to do is just explore. I kiss her again and I place my hand around her breast. I start to move my mouth down there as well, kissing her on the neck and licking her skin and running my fingers slowly round in circles, but there's no way I can carry on. My need to get inside her is so strong and urgent that I know it's no use trying to put it off any longer. I've got to tell her.

'I'm sorry, Julie . . .' I start off. I want to make my voice sound soft and romantic, but it comes out kind of cracked and squeaky. '. . . I want you too badly . . .'

Julie gives a sort of resigned nod. She doesn't look too happy about it. I reach underneath the pillow and take out the packet of contraceptives. I've got to concentrate on this and get it right. I turn away from Julie for a few seconds as I unroll a condom over me, pushing the base down properly and straightening it out. Then I turn back and put my arm around her and place my leg between hers. 'I really did want to make it good for you . . .' I mumble . . . 'but it'll have to wait until another time . . .'

Julie nods again, but she doesn't look enthusiastic. I kiss her passionately on the mouth, hoping to make her understand, then I lever myself on top of her, remembering to place my weight on my arms and elbows so she doesn't get completely flattened. I think that's the only thing I actually remember from all my manuals on the art of love. All the complicated descriptions about adventurous positions need never have been written as far as I'm concerned this afternoon.

Julie spreads her legs apart and it takes me a while to get inside her. I haven't even looked at her down there and the bits that I can feel don't seem to bear any relation to the dozens of diagrams I've studied. She uses her hand to guide me when I seem to be drilling holes in her body in places where holes shouldn't be. Inside her it feels tight and dry, and I know that that's because she isn't ready, but it's too late for anything like that to put me off. I start to move around inside her, still keeping the bulk of my weight away from her and kissing her hair and her ears and neck. I want to stop myself from coming. I know I could come straightaway if I gave up holding back and just let go, but I don't want it to be over just yet. I don't want Julie to realize that this is the first time I've ever made it with a girl.

I decide to try and divert my thoughts by thinking about the rally. I picture myself standing on the platform and try to remember my speech, but all I can recall are the first couple of lines. Then I hear the crowd applauding and the cheers and chanting and I realize that, instead of acting as a diversion, the sound in my head is spurring me on, forcing me to lose control, thrusting myself forward into the sea of noise, losing myself completely inside the enormous barrier of sound. I hear the audience applauding me and feel the vibrations of the stamping, chanting crowd as I finally lose myself inside a flood of throbbing blood vessels.

There's only one thing that spoils it for me. In the instant after climax, I see a sudden flash of Sarah's face, filling the screen of my mind with her beautiful hazel eyes, searing me with disappointment and disgust. For the second time this afternoon, she ruins my moment of triumph. I hate her for it.

I give a final angry thrust inside Julie. 'Fuck Sarah,' I mutter under my breath. Julie yelps with pain.

'I'm sorry.' I apologize straightaway. I never meant to hurt her. I lie on top of her, spent and gasping.

*

I leave Julie's house in a kind of daze and walk down to the bus-stop. The world around me is blurred and out of focus; everything is distant. I feel as though my mind is awash somewhere, floating underneath sensations that it didn't realize existed, trying to assimilate events it didn't know were possible. Sensations swim through my mind, thrashing their tails against my brain like a scurry of spermatozoa. A montage of scenes: the march, the crowds of people watching, shouting down the megaphone, the audience at the Civic Hall, my speech, the crowd applauding me, the pub afterwards . . . going to bed with Julie . . . and, superimposed across the footage, Sarah's face glaring at me with derision, shattering the frail facade of my success.

I try not to think about Sarah. I think instead about going to bed with Julie. Even though I feel bad about the fact that I didn't help her to enjoy it, and even though I never got round to using any of the exciting techniques I'd learned from *Coming Together* and *Making it Good*, the fact is that I made it. I made it. I made it. I feel worn out, knackered, half-drunk with the beer I'm not used to having swilling round my empty stomach. But in spite of that I feel good and complete and successful.

I close my eyes for a few seconds as I lean against the bus-stop and, as I stand waiting, and notice that it's turning cold, I realize that I've left my jacket behind. I think I left it somewhere in Julie's kitchen. I wonder if I've time to go back for it, but I can see the bus turning round the corner now and I know I'm going to be late home as it is. I haven't said anything to Julie about seeing her again, but leaving the jacket round there would be a good excuse for going back some time. I decide to leave it behind and catch the bus.

*

At home the salad's waiting ready on my plate. I still feel vague and slightly drunk as I sit down at the table like an alien from Andromeda and gaze at the pink pressed ham and hard-boiled egg gaping at me from the Spring Snot china. The egg begins to slowly pulsate like a giant throbbing eyeball and the ham keeps rising slightly and floating gently round the plate. I wish everything would keep still. I blink my eyes and stare at the table, struggling to keep all the major items in focus: the knife, the fork, a spring onion, but then the kitchen starts to slowly spin around and items begin to merge together like the view from the top of a Corkscrew.

'Did the procession go off all right?' I hear my mother's voice from somewhere on my right.

Procession! A huge great demo of twelve thousand people marching and chanting through the city centre and she calls it a procession! And what does she mean by *go off*? Launched off into space like a three-mile wide ballistic missile? Or *go off* like a four-week-old boiled egg? I find the strength to sip my tea and try to find words to communicate just a tiny fraction of what the demo was about, but I know it isn't worth it. I put down my cup and sigh. 'It was all right,' I tell her.

'I thought it looked as if it might rain earlier on,' my mother chunters, spearing her fork into her tomato .

I think about the Lord Mayor and his weather report and I nod my head in resignation. I concentrate on lifting up my knife and fork and cutting a slice off the thin end of a spring onion, but I can't find the incentive to pick it up and bring it near my mouth.

'It brightened up later on, though,' my dad reports.

I feel as if I don't belong here. I know who it is they think I am: the little boy they knew once who rushed off to join the Woodcraft Folk and who played the trombone in school concerts so they could toddle along and clap. The boy who wanted gnomes in the front garden and liked to sit on Daddy's knee and pretend to help him drive the car. They knew him once, that kid; but he doesn't live here any more. I don't know when they'll notice that he's gone.

I force myself to eat the salad. I nearly choke on it, but I can't cope with them fussing round me. I get it down me somehow and then I walk upstairs and go inside my room, shut the door and lie down on my bed.

It's a couple of hours now since I lay in bed with Julie, but the sensations haven't left me. They seep across my body in soft and saturating waves. I don't need to imagine that Julie's lying here beside me, or make up fantasies about her; I don't need to work out how it could have been better with her today. I just accept what's happened and let sensations ripple through me, wallowing in a hazy satisfaction.

13

I'm not in love with Julie; I know that. What I've got is what *Coming Together* describes as: 'physical attraction, where the man and woman haven't yet had time to share each other's private worlds . . . divulge their innermost secrets. Physical attraction can be a powerful driving force in human relationships, but it never achieves either the permanence or the unrivalled ecstasy of true reciprocated love . . .'

All I know is that if screwing Julie does things like this to my metabolism, they can keep the unrivalled ecstasy of love for now. I've got enough to cope with at the moment.

Today it's Sunday and I've been thinking about Julie all the time since yesterday. If it was an ordinary girl at school I'd screwed, I know she'd be really mad if I made out that was all I wanted and I didn't make any arrangements about seeing her again. With Julie though, I have the feeling that it might be all *she* wanted—that she wouldn't take too happily to the idea that we were going out together. Anyway, I've been lying awake half the night thinking about her and I'm still walking round the house like a zombie with amnesia, so I've decided that the only thing to do is catch the bus down to Summerfield Terrace and call and collect my jacket. It won't do any harm to just remind her who I am.

Julie opens the door, looking bleary-eyed and half-asleep. She looks as though she hasn't been up too long. She's wearing a long, matted cardigan that looks like one of the leftovers from the Revival Hall Worzel Gummidge stall and jeans that are held together by a safety-pin. She doesn't seem surprised to see me. 'Hi,' she says. 'Come in.'

I walk into the kitchen. The mess is still the same as it was yesterday, but the smell is getting worse. I take a gasp of fresh air before Julie closes the door behind me.

'Do you want some coffee?'

I look at the unwashed coffee mugs balanced on the draining-board. Two of them have been used as ashtrays and the rest have chip grease smeared around the edges. I shake my head. 'No, thanks,' I tell her.

'O.K. We're just having a meeting,' Julie tells me. 'You'd better come on through.'

I try not to show my disappointment that we can't just leap into bed together. Perhaps there'll be time for that afterwards. I walk behind her into the front room, where the air is thick with smoke, the curtains are closed and the lights are on, even though it's sunny outside. I say hello to Mike, Ralph and Trevor who are sprawled around the floor, looking at pieces of paper and a map. I find a space on the carpet and sit down. Lying at the other end of the carpet is a leather jacket. It looks like mine, but it has metal studs across the back.

Julie spreads out the jacket so that I can see it properly. 'What do you think?' she asks me.

Across the back of the jacket are big block letters made from metal studs. They spell out the name of the Action Group: D.A.M.N. I don't know what to say. My first reaction is that she's got no right to mess about with my jacket without so much as asking me. I glance around the circle of faces watching me and then look across at Julie, proudly showing off the jacket. I don't want to offend her. 'It's great,' I tell her. 'Did you do it?'

Julie grins. 'Yes,' she answers. 'I found a box of studs at the back of one of the drawers when I moved in here. I've been waiting for something to put them on.'

She lays the jacket on the threadbare carpet, and I walk across and kneel beside it. Tentatively, I trace my fingers over the silver heads of the three-sided metal studs. They feel cold and hard to touch. The light reflects on them from the unshaded bulb on the ceiling.

I pick up my jacket, try it on, turning round so that everyone can see the back. 'How's it look?' I ask them.

'Great.'

'Fantastic.'

I run my hands along the familiar worn black leather, then I turn around and face Julie again. 'Thanks,' I tell her. 'It looks great.' I keep the jacket on as I sit down on the carpet and join in with the meeting.

'I'll recap on what I was saying earlier on, Chris,' says

Ralph. 'Then you can understand what's happening.'

'So . . .' He points at the map in front of him and traces his finger across what looks like a spiral of squashed spaghetti. 'We assemble at grid reference 860908,' he explains, 'then proceed in a north-easterly direction towards this trig point here . . .' He points his finger at a semi-circle that looks like a diagrammatic cross-section of a sheep's brain. 'We then synchronize watches, review weather conditions and camouflage all vehicles before proceeding due north to rendezvous at 1100 hours at this key communications site . . . here.' He pauses and looks up at me. 'All right, Chris?'

I don't know how to tell him that I can't understand a word he's saying. I frown studiously and move my fingers over my chin like a professor stroking an imaginary beard. 'What's a key communications site?' I ask.

'A telephone box.'

'Oh.'

'Assembled wings will then advance towards the base here, with the strategic objective of occupation followed by disabling action.'

Assembled wings to me are things you make out of Airfix kits. I wish he'd start explaining things in English.

'Should there be an occasion for strategic withdrawal, sections will follow this easting . . .' he traces his finger over a vertical line on the page . . . 'to the less easily accessible rural location here, where re-grouping will commence in readiness for an escalation of the offensive.'

I want to ask an intelligent question like what to do if it's raining. It takes me nearly half a minute to work out how to phrase it. 'What would be our course of action on the occasion of a large amount of precipitation?' I ask him.

Ralph frowns at me quizzically. 'You mean if it's raining?'

'Yes.'

'We'd get wet,' says Trevor.

'Oh.' Perhaps I ought to keep my mouth shut. When I'm actually wandering round the spaghetti spirals and clambering up and down the sliced sheep's brain, I suppose it'll all just fall into place.

'Any more questions?'

I want to find out when all this is supposed to be happening. I just wish I knew whether I ought to ask questions in English or not. 'On what occasions are these . . . er . . . manoeuvres occurring?' I ask. 'Is this advance planning of . . . er . . . a long-term future campaign strategy or . . . is it some time this week?'

Mike lights up two cigarettes and passes one across to me. 'It's a surprise attack,' he explains. 'Whenever there's been any aggro so far, we've been outnumbered by the cops by about three to one. So this time, we're not letting people know until the morning we set off. All we should be up against then are a few dozen local bobbies. We ought to be able to knock that lot flying like a set of skittles.'

'How will we find out when it's happening, then?'

'We use the telephone tree,' says Mike.

'Oh.' I imagine a massive tree with telephones clustered like bananas on its branches, their wires trailing round the trunk like liquorice tendrils.

Julie can see that I'm looking puzzled. 'We all have a list of contacts,' she explains. 'Five or six others to get in touch with, if we want to call people out. One person phones about six people and they all call six others—or they go round and see people who aren't on the phone. We can get stacks of people out in just a few hours.'

'Ralph's expecting a call about half six on the morning of the Action,' Mike explains. 'That'll give us an hour to phone round and get organized. It means we've all to be on the alert every morning this week and get ready with only about half an hour's notice.'

'Can you handle that, Chris?' Ralph asks me.

I'm supposed to be at school next week, but it'll be great to take a day off when the other kids are working. The plan sounds good as well. I can only understand little bits and pieces of all that Ralph's been saying, but it's obvious that he's got it tightly organized. It sounds professional, like a proper military exercise. The idea I had about D.A.M.N. before was that it was just groups of amateurs without any proper organization, but with people like Ralph running operations, I can see it in a different light.

'Right. Anything else?' Ralph asks, looking round.

Mike glances across at me. 'You'll need some protection, Chris,' he tells me. He looks at my trainers and shakes his head. 'You'll want something on your feet for starters. Have you got any boots?'

I have some Doc Martens at home, but I don't wear them much. 'Yes,' I tell him. 'I'll wear my Doc Martens.'

'I'll phone Chris, if you like,' says Trevor. 'I've only got four numbers.' It's not often that Trevor says anything and it always surprises me that he speaks so quietly. He's such a big bloke, you'd expect him to have a voice like a gorilla. 'What's your number, Chris?'

I write my number on a piece of paper and pass it across to him.

'So,' says Ralph, 'we'll go through the itinerary: initial communication links to be established at 0600 hours, then telephone tree to be put into operation. Vehicle owners to receive first notice of engagement and to rendezvous as previously detailed . . .'

'O.K.' Everyone nods as if they understand. I nod and say O.K. as well, although I can hardly work out what he's on about.

'All communications to use the code name Operation Badger and the *noms de guerre* . . . Ravioli . . .' He looks at Julie.

'Jam Sandwich.'

'Toasted Teacake,' says Trevor.

'Marmalade,' says Mike.

'Chris?'

They all turn round and look at me. I've worked out that it's like a party game where you have to say the name of a food beginning with the first letter of your name. 'Cottage Pie . . . ?' I suggest.

'Great. So if Cottage Pie can rendezvous with the vehicle at 0758 at grid reference 240679 which is approximately four kilometres due south of the junction of the . . .'

'I'm not sure where you mean,' I interrupt.

'You know that chip shop at the bottom of Hagg Farm Lane . . . ?' Trevor asks me.

'The one on the main road?'

'Yes. We're meeting there.'

'Oh good.' Although I don't see why they shouldn't have told me that in the first place.

'So, you'll all come prepared,' says Ralph. 'Conditions could be hazardous and you may need some protection.'

I'll bring my cagoule and maybe a pair of wellies. I can always leave them in this vehicle if it isn't raining or anything.

'Is the off-licence open?' Ralph asks Julie.

'Should be.'

'Will you fetch us some cigarettes, then. I've just run out.'

Julie hesitates. She's obviously not keen on being asked to run errands for people, but doesn't want to say no to Ralph.

'I'll go, if you like,' I offer, starting to get up.

Mike takes hold of my arm and pulls me back. 'Let Julie go,' he says quietly.

I don't see why I should. It would have been O.K. for us both to have gone to the shop, especially if it meant getting something established about going to bed together again. And it would be nice if we could still find time for that this afternoon.

I sit back down as Ralph takes out his wallet and passes Julie some cash. 'Go out the back way,' he tells her.

'O.K.'

Ralph walks with Julie to the door that leads to the kitchen. He rests his hand on her shoulder and says something to her quietly. I have a feeling that he's telling her to take her time. Julie nods understandingly before she walks away.

Ralph walks back and joins us on the floor. 'Right, let's get on with the other item on the agenda,' he says. 'Sarah Barnforth.'

Mike swears underneath his breath.

'We're bound to have problems with Sarah,' Ralph says, 'now she's living here permanently.'

Trevor shakes his head in disgust. 'I put up with Sarah,' he grumbles, 'just the way you told us to—talked to her nicely and sold her copies of *Action* and all that stuff. But when she went on the radio . . .' He shakes his head again.

'What happened?' I ask him.

'One of the local radio blokes phoned up to ask for her dad's comments about the last D.A.M.N. Day of Action. Her dad wasn't in so Sarah did all the bloody interview herself and claimed she was speaking on behalf of the local peace movement. She said that they completely disassociated themselves from us. Nobody'd told her to say it or anything. It was disgusting.'

'Worst of it was when everybody said what a brilliant job she'd made of it. They never stopped praising her.'

'I bet you were livid.'

'*Livid?*' says Mike, squashing out his cigarette with such force that the filter is completely flattened. 'We were so livid that we thought about piling round there and shoving her underneath a bus!'

'Anyway,' says Ralph, 'what I'm suggesting is that we ask Chris to try and chat Sarah up a bit. He's about the same age as she is and he's not bad-looking. He might just get her interested . . .'

It's odd the way they're talking about me almost as if I'm not there. I just grin at them stupidly. I don't see any way that I can chat up Sarah.

'No chance.' Mike interrupts him. 'Sarah's as stubborn as they come. He'll never get anywhere.'

'Well, it won't hurt to try,' says Ralph. For the first time he turns and addresses this part of the conversation to me. 'If you just go round and see her a few times, Chris . . . go out with her a bit . . . you know, try and talk her round. You know what I mean . . .'

'It's a waste of time,' Mike says again. 'An absolute waste of time. We could use him better doing something else.'

'We can let him have a go,' says Ralph. 'You'll be all right, Chris, won't you?'

It doesn't occur to any of them that Sarah is so far out of my class that I can hardly bring myself to talk to her. I nod at Ralph. 'O.K.' I tell him. 'I'll have a go.'

'I'll tell you what,' says Ralph. 'Bevan Barnforth was moaning about how the leaflets we put out for the rally yesterday didn't put across the policy of the peace movement and all that garbage. What about me phoning Sarah up and suggesting that you and she work together on the next leaflet? You could go round and see her and talk about it . . .'

'Sounds O.K.'

'It'll be a lead-in, anyway, won't it?'

Mike looks at us in disgust. 'Come on. Let's get a pint in before they shut.' He glances at his watch. 'We've got half an hour left.'

'Are you coming down the pub, Chris?' Ralph asks me as they get to their feet.

I do want to go to bed with Julie again and I think that might be difficult anyway; it'll be impossible when I'm at the pub. 'No thanks,' I tell them. 'I'll stay on here and tidy up.'

'O.K. We'll be seeing you then, Chris.'

Ralph hasn't even waited to get his cigarettes from Julie.

'Cheers.'

They go out the back way through the kitchen.

There isn't much to do when the others have gone—Julie doesn't seem to have any books or records or anything—so I decide to do my good deed for the month and make a start on her five-day supply of washing-up.

The kitchen is even worse when you look at it on your own. My first job is to open the door wide—I try the windows but they're moulded to the frames with dirt and grease. I put the kettle on to boil and start to clear the piles of filthy crockery out of the sink. As well as the pots, there are soggy fag-ends floating on the greasy water, several smelly tea bags, a dozen or so dead chips and a crushed carton of congealed curry sauce.

When I've ladled the debris out of the sink, I have to scour out the washing-up bowl, but before I can do that, I have to scald the smelly dish-cloth. I keep expecting Julie to come back, but she's obviously taking her time. I hope she hasn't met the others and gone off to the pub.

Actually, I don't mind washing-up. My mother assumes that women have this extra gene that makes them intrinsically better at washing-up than men and I'm usually only allowed to dry the pots at home. I think that's stupid and I think it's daft as well for Julie to leave her washing-up to get this bad. I'm just finishing off, when she walks in through the door with two carrier-bags full of shopping. 'Hi.'

'Hi.'

She glances disparagingly at the piles of sparkling crockery. 'You've been busy,' she comments.

'Yes,' I tell her. The least she could have said is thank you.

'Haven't you made any coffee?'

How could I have made coffee as well, when I've been so busy? What does she think I am? 'I'll put the kettle on,' I offer.

I'm expecting Julie to get out the coffee and stuff, but she doesn't. She just sits down and lights up a cigarette, while she watches me finish scouring out the frying-pan.

I don't quite know why it is, but I don't feel as relaxed with Julie now we're on our own together. I try really hard to think of something to say to her but when I've thought of things, they don't seem right and I can't bring myself to say them. I try to cover up by humming casually to myself as I hunt around for a towel. The only cloth I can find looks as though it's been used to wipe up an avalanche of curry sauce. Or vomit. I wipe my hands dry on my jeans instead.

Even the humming doesn't sound right. Instead of the sound just flowing down my nostrils, I get this kind of nasal constipation. It takes an enormous effort to force the vibrations through my nose, and the musical hum I'd hoped for squalls out like a stifled fart. I clear my throat awkwardly and make the coffee, asking Julie if she wants milk and sugar and easy stuff like that.

'Thanks.' She takes the mug of coffee from me, but doesn't say anything else. What I want is to ask her whether she'd like to go to bed with me again, but I can't think how to introduce it into the conversation.

'You're nearly out of washing-up liquid,' I tell her.

Julie nods at me with the excited expression on her face that people have sitting watching cheese go mouldy.

Part of me feels tempted to just give up and go back home, but I desperately want to have sex with her again, even if it's only one more time. 'You're low on scouring-powder as well,' I mention. 'I nearly used it all on that frying-pan.'

Julie doesn't look up. She sighs and then stubs out her cigarette on a cardboard chip tray left lying on the table. 'Are we going to bed, then, or not?' she asks me.

I choke slightly on my coffee, but I know it's as well that she's said it. I'd only have finished up talking drivel for the rest of the afternoon.

'O.K.' I tell her, downing my coffee. I try to make it sound really casual as though the idea had never even occurred to me until she said it. I spoil the effect by nearly tripping over the kitchen stool in my eagerness to follow Julie out of the kitchen and up the stairs.

In some ways, things are better. Having sex with Julie isn't quite as urgent as it was before and I manage to keep the brakes on better. I don't feel scared this time that I won't be able to do it. On the other hand, it's not as good. I work really hard to recover the intensity of feeling that I had yesterday—the sense of power and elation. The crowds applauding me and cheering, the volume of sound echoing inside my head. I tell myself that I'm a winner, that there's nothing I can't do. I tell myself that Julie's panting for me, yearning and ecstatic. But her body lies beneath me cold and rigid; her face is passive and expressionless. And still, when I close my eyes, I see Sarah's face dissecting me. Rebuking me. Making me feel small and hurt. And it's the anger I feel again at Sarah that brings me to a climax, pounding into Julie the uneasy rage I feel for someone else. I wish I were screwing Sarah.

After we've finished, Julie reaches across for her cigarettes and matches and lights us both a cigarette. I didn't intend to carry on smoking after I'd finished the packet I bought yesterday, but it doesn't seem right to tell her even a simple thing like that. I don't mind really because smoking a cigarette afterwards at least gives me something to do. I know it's not right just to leap straight out of bed as soon as I've finished and run down the street to catch the bus (after I've got dressed, that is) and yet lying in bed with her is awkward because there doesn't seem anything more we have to do.

I inhale on the cigarette and gaze at the cracks and cobwebs on the ceiling. There are lots of things I'd have liked Julie to do to me, but there was no way I could bring myself to ask her. There are things I would have liked to do as well that might have made it better for Julie, but it doesn't seem right to talk about them. It seems silly really, because although I feel as though I know Julie well enough to go to bed with her, I don't feel as though I know her well enough for us to talk to each other properly.

I put out my cigarette and then reach across and kiss Julie on the cheek before I climb out of bed and start searching for my clothes. I don't think Julie's all that keen on me, anyway. I get dressed and put on my jacket. I don't mind about the studs now. I think they look good.

I say good-bye to Julie and go out to catch the bus.

14

The phone rings on Monday evening. 'Hello, is Chris there, please?'

'Speaking.'

'Hi. It's Sarah Barnforth.'

'Hi. Nice to hear from you.'

'Ralph phoned me yesterday about the leaflets for the next meeting. He thought you and I could work together on putting something out. Has he talked about it with you?'

'Yes, he did mention something about it.'

'What do you think?'

'Sounds O.K. We might not agree on everything . . .'

'That's what I said, but Ralph thought we'd get more of a balance if we both worked on it. That's what he said, anyway.'

'Sounds a good idea. When shall we get together?'

'There are piles of stuff I'll have to do for school later on this week. What about tonight? Are you busy?'

'No. That'll be best for me actually. I'll be busy later in the week.' Pause. 'Shall I come round to your place?'

'Mmm . . . yes, all right. I don't want to put you out . . .'

'No, that's O.K. It'll be nice to get out of the house for a while. Ralph's given me your address.'

'Will you be able to find it O.K.?'

'I should think so.'

'There are only three houses in the street. Ours is right at the end.'

'O.K. I'll find it. I'll be round in about an hour.'
'O.K. See you later.'
'Bye.'
'Bye.'

I walk down the centre of the unpaved road, knowing there will be no traffic. It's turning dusk now and the sun is casting long, low shadows. The air is quiet except for the singing of birds. On either side of me the trees grow tall and heavy with a canopy of leaves that are just beginning to turn gold. The road is so peaceful and calm and enclosed that it's almost like entering a church. It's like a kind of sanctuary.

It's quite a long street, considering it only has three houses. The first house, on the corner, has a notice to say that it's the premises of a Pentecostal Church, but it looks as though it's only used on Sundays. The second house is empty and derelict. It has rusty iron gates on which the padlock has been smashed apart. The gates are swinging open on their hinges, creaking with a sound like someone crying. A soft whimper like the voice of a woman or a child.

The Barnforth house is large and made of stone. I ring the bell and stand gazing round at the garden as I wait. In front of me is a lawn, bordered with shrubs and bushes and with an old-fashioned summer house standing in the corner.

I felt nervous before about seeing Sarah. Now I feel calm and resolute, conscious of the mission, assured that what I have to do is right and necessary.

Sarah answers the door. She's wearing blue denim jeans and a shirt made of white Indian muslin—the sort you think you could see through if you scrutinized it long enough. 'Hi.' She smiles at me. 'Come on in.'

I follow her through a panelled hallway into a room which looks out over the back garden. The late evening sun is shining through the french windows. The room is filled with books from floor to ceiling.

'It's a fantastic house,' I say.

She smiles at me. 'I like it,' she tells me.

She pulls a large file from a desk in the corner and extracts some papers. 'I've drawn up some ideas already,' she says, 'though I think I might have written too much. I'm not sure how to cut it down.'

I wait for Sarah to sit down, then I sit opposite her, taking off my leather jacket and folding it neatly over the arm of the chair. I want her to be impressed with me. I've no intention of criticizing whatever ideas she has for the leaflet. It would be useful if we could produce something that was good publicity for D.A.M.N., but that's not important at the moment. The essential thing is working with Sarah and getting her to trust me, so that I can tell her more about D.A.M.N. and why our campaign is so important.

Sarah passes her papers across to me and I start to read through them. The room is very quiet except for a few birds still singing outside. I feel very conscious of Sarah looking at me as I read through the neatly typewritten sheets and I struggle hard to concentrate. I've read through the whole of the first sheet before I realize that I've no idea at all what it's about. All that I'm aware of is that I'm in the room with Sarah, that we're alone together, that this is Sarah's house I've entered, making myself a part of her life and the birds are still singing outside. The words in front of me are printed patterns on a piece of paper.

'It's very good,' I tell her. Then I realize there are two more sheets I haven't even looked at. 'I think you're right about the length, though,' I add.

'Which part do you think could be left out?'

I wave my hand vaguely across the whole of the three sheets. 'Well . . . bits here and there . . .'

'Which points do you think we should concentrate on, then . . . ?'

We kneel down together on the carpet and work through the leaflet line by line. We don't have any problems talking to each other, but I'm aware of something between us like an invisible electric fence. I don't touch Sarah and I don't look her directly in the face. I inspect her hands and her long, slim fingers pencilling alterations to the typescript. I notice her neck which is pale and slender and, when her attention is distracted, I find myself gazing at her frail, white shirt, hoping to distinguish the shape of her body underneath.

'Would you mind passing me the pencil sharpener, please? It's just at the side of you.'

Even with an object as small as a pencil sharpener, we make sure that our fingers never touch.

'Thank you.'

After a while, there's a knock on the door and Sarah's father walks in.

'Hello there—Chris, isn't it?'

I stand up and shake hands with him. I did think he wouldn't want me to associate with Sarah after hearing the speech I made at the rally, but he doesn't look as if he minds my being here. He looks quite genial.

'That's right. How do you do?'

He nods at me, then turns to Sarah. 'I've just made some coffee,' he tells her. 'Haven't you offered Chris a drink?'

Sarah looks apologetic. 'I'll fetch some in for us,' she says, leaving the room.

She returns with a jug and mugs and pours out the coffee. I stand and survey the book-lined walls and the desk piled high with *Marxism Today*.

'I told Ralph I wasn't happy about that leaflet your group produced for the rally,' says Mr Barnforth. I notice Sarah glancing at her dad with disapproval, but he doesn't take any notice. 'I wondered what you thought about it, Chris . . .'

'Well . . .' There's an awkward silence as I stumble to think of something vague and non-committal to say. Sarah helps me out. 'Chris was very busy that morning,' she tells her father. 'He might not have had time to read the leaflet . . .'

'That's true. I mean, I did notice that the leaflets all had D.A.M.N. logos on them and, personally, I don't think that was a good idea, but . . .'

'Time's running out, you know, Chris.' Mr Barnforth shakes his head in disapproval. 'We mustn't build up antagonism against the movement. We can't afford to do anything that'll lose us mass support.'

'Chris *does* know that,' Sarah interrupts. 'He's come here to help me work on a new leaflet.' She speaks to her dad reprovingly, but lightheartedly. I wish I could talk to my father like that. 'We were doing all right till you came in.'

Her father nods understandingly. 'O.K.,' he says. 'I'll let you get on with it.' He turns to leave the room. 'Hope to see you again, Chris,' he tells me.

When we get back to work, Sarah seems more relaxed, as if she's beginning to feel more at ease with me. Instead of sitting upright and cross-legged, she starts to lounge around a little, leaning backwards with her weight on the arm of a chair. When the leaflet's finished, she rocks gently backwards, drinking the last of her coffee. We look each other full in the face for what is probably the first time since I came here. 'I'm sorry about my dad butting in,' she says.

'That's all right. He's a nice bloke.'

'The peace movement is very important to him.'

'It's important to me as well.'

Sarah hesitates for a moment. 'My father's always been wary of fanaticism,' she explains. 'He knows it won't do the peace movement any good.'

I look across at the huge pile of *Marxism Today* and the rows of shelves filled with books on socialism. 'Isn't he a fanatic?' I ask her.

Sarah shakes her head. 'No,' she answers quietly. 'My father's dedicated, but he isn't a fanatic.'

'What's the difference?'

Sarah puts down her coffee mug. 'My father became a Marxist because he has a deep respect for people,' she explains. 'He believes that, if people are able to improve their living conditions and gain control over their own lives, then they can become caring and responsible and . . . autonomous.'

I'm not sure what *autonomous* means and I don't understand what all of this has to do with D.A.M.N. I shrug my shoulders. 'So . . . ?'

Sarah pauses. 'My father would never support an organization which didn't treat people with respect,' she goes on. 'He could never throw a petrol bomb at a policeman. He sees policemen as ordinary men inside a uniform. You can't throw bombs at a uniform and miss the man inside.'

I don't think Sarah understands. 'None of us *want* to hurt people,' I tell her, 'but it sometimes has to come to that to produce good in the end. You have to do obnoxious things sometimes, so you can bring about the things you know will be valuable.'

Sarah shakes her head. 'History judges any movement,' she tells me, 'not on its aims, but on the means it takes to achieve them. If you belong to a terrorist organization, then society judges you as murderers, no matter how high-minded your ideals are . . .'

'But we're not terrorists,' I interrupt her. 'We're not doing anything like that . . .'

'It could come to that. People could get killed.'

'But everybody in the whole of the bloody world'll get killed if we don't do something to stop it.' I feel angry that Sarah should be so stubborn.

She shakes her head. 'The leaders of the Spanish Inquisition thought their methods were justified,' she answers calmly. 'They believed that they were saving people's souls.'

I think for a minute, but I don't know enough about the Spanish Inquisition to argue with her. Perhaps I ought to be going. I struggle to think how I can arrange to see Sarah again. 'I could call round when the sheets are re-typed,' I offer. 'I'll take them to the printers, if you like.'

'O.K.,' says Sarah. 'I'll phone you when they're ready.'

'Fine.' I pause. 'I'd better be going now.'

I'd like to say something nice to her before I leave. Something subtle that she can think about when I've gone, but nothing occurs to me. I put my mug down on the table and think about touching Sarah. I think about kissing her lightly on the cheek before I go or just putting my arm around her waist, but I don't want to do anything that might put her off me.

I pick up my jacket and follow Sarah to the door. On the front step I hesitate. 'Thanks for asking me round,' I tell her.

'That's O.K.'

'And for the coffee as well.'

'It's a pleasure.'

I've paused too long now for any gesture towards her to look spontaneous. 'I'll see you later on in the week some time . . .'

'O.K.'

Before I move down the steps, I raise my hand and touch her gently on the arm. That's all. Sarah doesn't shrink away from me; she grasps my hand for a tiny fraction of a second before she walks back into the house.

'Good-night, Chris.'

'Bye.'

I walk down the driveway towards the darkened street.

15

I can think about nothing else but Operation Badger. I get up early each morning for the next few days and polish my shoes for half an hour, standing by the telephone. All the time, I feel high and excited, wanting the phone to ring so I can snatch it up before my mother comes downstairs, but dreading it as well, because I don't really know what's going to happen. When I go to school, I'm conscious of the fact that I'm living on a different plane from everyone else. The other kids have crises in their lives, like they've lost one of their football socks or their sponge cake's gone sad in the middle. I talk away to them about all the usual boring stuff and never let on that now I'm a member of D.A.M.N.—that I'm walking around with all kinds of secret information in my head about code names and key communications sites. It makes me feel very important.

What I've worked out is that we're going to make for a

missile base that's near a village called Bedgar. I saw that on the map that Ralph was studying. I've looked it up in my father's A.A. book and it's about sixty or seventy miles away from here. Operation Badger must be an anagram. I like the idea of everything being kept secret—only Ralph receiving information about the plans, closed meetings with the curtains drawn, always leaving the house by the back door, even the silly code names . . .

The phone rings on Wednesday at seven o'clock in the morning. I pick it up within half a second. 'Hi, Chris here.'

There's a pause for a moment or two. 'Cottage Pie . . . ?'

'Yes . . . sorry . . . affirmative.'

'This is Toasted Teacake.' That means it's Trevor. 'Rendezvous at 0758, as previously detailed.'

'Outside the chip shop?'

'Yes . . . er . . . affirmative.'

I'll have to hurry up. My mother'll be coming downstairs to cook breakfast soon. 'O.K. Willco.'

'Pardon?'

'Wil . . . oh, never mind. Are there any further instructions?' Pause. 'Over.'

I wish he'd get a move on. I can hear the toilet flushing and the padding of hand-knitted slippers across the landing. My mother'll be down here any minute.

'You'll have to bring something with you, Chris. You know . . . come prepared.'

'O.K.' My mother's hand-knitted feet are now waddling down the stairs. They'll be turning the corner any second. 'All right,' I tell him. 'I'll see you. Over and out.'

I replace the receiver almost soundlessly and scurry into the kitchen, just before my mother rounds the corner.

I find it hard to behave normally as I watch her cook the breakfast. I don't seem able to stand still for very long, so I start humming tunes and clicking my fingers and rearranging the cereal packets into interesting shapes on the table.

I'm not sure what Trevor meant about preparations. I've got a bag upstairs with my cagoule and wellies in it, but perhaps I ought to take some food as well. With all this split-second timing we probably won't have time to stop at a café on the way. I wish I'd thought about it before because, since we don't have any variations in the menu at our house, we never have spare food. Today's Wednesday and that's fried eggs, so I could sidle some slices of toast and an egg into a plastic bag. I've never eaten a completely cold fried egg before, but, when the future of the human race is at stake, I don't suppose I should worry over minor details like that.

I sneak a freezer bag out of the cupboard. Then I sit with it on my knee and surreptitiously slide slices of peanut-buttered toast inside it. The egg's more difficult. First of all, I have to balance it on the edge of my plate, then check there's no one watching. My father's range of vision extends no further than the Rupert Bear column in this morning's *Daily Express* and my mother's absorbing the instructions on the back of the Sugar Softies for knitting your own hovercraft out of yogurt tops and spaghetti. I launch the fried egg into a back flip with my fork. I'm glad it's been cooked on both sides because it lands on the chair seat in between my legs. It could have been really messy if the yolk had still been runny. I drink my tea with one hand and, with the other, manoeuvre the egg from between my legs and ease it into the plastic bag. I try to land it neatly on top of the toast, but it dollops down to the bottom of the plastic bag, crumpled like a clapped-out goldfish.

My mother gazes at my empty plate. 'You shouldn't eat so quickly, Christopher,' she grumbles. 'You'll get indigestion.'

I can't count the number of times she's told me that and I've never had indigestion in my life. 'I'm in a rush this morning,' I explain. 'The bus has been arriving early. I don't want to miss it.'

I walk upstairs and hide my school bag under the bed. I swap it for the bag with the wellies and cagoule in and place my lunch in there as well. I put my leather jacket over my arm with the lining on the outside. My parents haven't seen the studs yet.

'I'll probably be home late,' I shout as I head towards the door. 'There's an extra chess match on this week.'

I don't wait to hear their answer as I close the door behind me. I lift up my bag as I walk past the G.T. San Marino. My dad goes mad if anything brushes against it and takes the shine off the polish.

I walk out into the street. Reporting for duty at 0758 on Operation Badger . . . here comes Cottage Pie.

When Ralph spoke about 'the vehicle' for Operation Badger I was assuming that we'd have a specially camouflaged, four-wheel-drive job, complete with CB radio and stuff. I can hardly believe it when his wrecked-up old Mini-van pulls into the lay-by near the chip shop. The nearside back tyre looks completely flat and the whole of the van is festooned with stickers saying things like:

```
END THE
ARMS RACE
   NOT
THE HUMAN RACE
```

I clamber into the front passenger seat, which is pushed so near the dashboard I have to crouch with my knees up next to my chin. By the time we arrive in Bedgar, I can see my limbs getting set in position and them having to shove me to the missile base in a wheelchair.

'We'll swap over in a bit,' says Ralph, 'and let somebody else have the seat. It's a bit cramped in the back.'

I look over my shoulder at Trevor's enormous square head looming like a close-up in a horror film. Behind him I think are Mike and Julie, but all I can see are patches of denim and boots.

'What did you all bring with you?' Ralph asks.

I don't really see why my lunch should have to be open to inspection, but I start to undo my freezer bag and take out the toast and egg.

'I thought this might be useful,' says Trevor. He holds out his massive, hairy hands and pays out a length of heavy chain that looks like a werewolf-lead.

'I brought these.' Mike leans forward and thrusts out his fists. His knuckles are covered with two black leather-studded wristbands. My stomach churns over slightly.

'What about you then, Chris?' asks Ralph.

I look down at the fried egg dangling between my thumb and finger. It doesn't look the kind of weapon to strike fear into the hearts of the U.S. Military. I drop it back quickly inside its plastic bag. 'I didn't want to get done for carrying an offensive weapon,' I explain.

The others nod understandingly as Ralph puts the engine into gear.

'The back tyre's flat,' I say to him before we set off.

'Don't worry,' says Julie. 'It's just Trev sitting on top of the wheel.'

Ralph revs up the engine and we start off, kangaroo-jumping down the road, making metallic scraping sounds. 'I think we might have a flat tyre,' says Ralph at last. 'I'd better have a look.'

He comes back five seconds later. 'Everybody out,' he orders. 'We've got a puncture.'

Ralph sets his stopwatch as everyone piles out of the van. 'We should be able to change a tyre in three to four minutes,' he explains. He looks disgustedly at the way everyone's wedged into different crouching positions through being cramped up in the van. They're jumping up and down on the grass verge like a set of Airfix pilots on springs, trying to straighten out.

'Right. Action stations!' Ralph calls, still looking at his watch. 'Toasted Teacake—remove the hub cap, then find the wheel brace and be loosening the wing nuts. Marmalade—you find the jack, place in position and commence levitation of the vehicle. Jam Sandwich—remove excess material from the rear of the vehicle. Find the spare wheel and place it ready for use. Cottage Pie . . .'

'I'll help Jam Sandwich,' I offer. I can't understand why Ralph has to use code names all the time. It's not that anyone's likely to be listening.

I help Julie clear the debris out of the van. There's a couple of sleeping-bags and fifty or sixty out-of-date copies of *Action*, as well as the expected pile of empty beer cans, squashed cigarette packets and torn maps. There's no spare wheel.

'It must be somewhere else in a Mini,' I tell her.

'Like where? Hanging from the roof? Squashed inside the radiator?'

'In my dad's car it's underneath,' I explain, 'in a gadget called an easy-access cradle.'

'We'd better have a look, then.'

I bend down and slide underneath the van. Trevor, at the same time, is prising off the hub cap. The van judders and a shower of rust falls into my eyes. 'Watch out!' I yell. Opening my mouth is stupid because an avalanche of rusted Mini, hardened bits of mud and other unmentionable debris cascades straight down my throat. I slither out from beneath the van, coughing and spitting and trying not to rub my eyes.

'I can't find a jack anywhere,' Mike's complaining.

'That's O.K.,' says Trev. 'I'll lift the van up. It doesn't weigh much.'

Through my half-closed eyes I see Trevor lifting up the side of the Mini-van as if it's a cardboard cut-out and holding it in mid-air. 'Hurry up and get the wheel off,' he's telling Mike. 'Somebody get the spare ready. Come on!'

'Three minutes . . . twenty-four seconds . . .'

'There isn't one,' I splutter.

'I'm not standing here like this all day. My arms'll drop off!'

'Three minutes . . . forty seconds.'

By this time, Mike's taken off the wheel and is rolling it out of the way. 'Hurry up,' Trevor complains. 'Get the spare wheel out!'

'There isn't one!' Julie and I both yell.

Trevor lets down the van and everybody searches for the non-existent spare wheel in all sorts of ludicrous places. Ralph keeps moaning about how we'll have to hurry up because of all the time we've lost, but it doesn't do any good. We can't make a spare wheel materialize out of thin air and there isn't a garage for miles. I sit down on the grass verge and try to get the rest of the rust from my eyes with one of Julie's tissues.

Ralph paces up and down, continually checking his stopwatch and getting more and more agitated. 'We'll have to nick one,' he says at last.

Trevor laughs. 'Where from? There are no car-parks round here and we can't take one from somebody's drive. They'd be coming out any minute and setting off for work.'

We all stare in resignation at the long stream of cars

pulling out one at a time to overtake the lop-sided Mini.

'We'll have to find one from somewhere,' says Ralph. 'Our section should be the advance wing. We have to rendezvous at 1100 hours with section . . .'

'Didn't you say your dad had a car?' Julie asks me.

'Oh yeah. A G.T. San Marino,' I laugh. 'I don't think he'd lend us that, somehow!'

The others turn and look at me. 'Doesn't he go to work in it?' asks Trevor.

'No, he leaves it in the drive.'

'Are there any keys in the house?'

'Yes, they're hanging up in the hall, but . . .'

'That sounds O.K.,' says Ralph. 'A G.T. San Marino —there'll be room for five of us in there, Chris, won't there?'

'Yes, but . . .' There's no way they can borrow the car. My dad nearly has a nervous breakdown if he gets bird droppings on his ancillary driving-lamps. How could I tell him that we'd just borrowed his car for the day to storm a missile base? 'My father'd go mad . . .' I start explaining.

'We'll bring it back,' says Ralph. 'What time does he get home from work?'

'Half past five.'

'That's O.K. We'll have time to clean it up and put some petrol in, if that makes you feel any better.'

'That's not the point. My mother'll be in all day and she'll . . .'

'Does she need the car?'

I suggested that my mother learn to drive when Dad started teaching me. *Don't be silly*, she said. *Women don't drive cars*. I suppose she thinks that the women drivers who pass our house just get shoved off down the street by their husbands and cling on to the steering-wheel with their feet in the air until they reach the Co-op.

'No, my mother doesn't drive, but she won't let me take the car. She'd . . .'

Julie walks across and puts her arm around my waist. 'Does it have reclining seats?' she asks me.

'Of course it does.'

'And one of those nice, long, comfy back seats?'

I know what she's suggesting but there's no way I could sit necking in the back seat of my father's car whilst Ralph or anyone else was driving it. 'I'd have to drive it myself,' I explain. 'I'd have to be responsible for it.'

'That's all right,' says Ralph. 'We don't mind letting Chris drive, do we?'

'No.'

'Is that O.K., then, Chris?' Ralph asks me. 'You and Trev can pick it up whilst the rest of us move the van out of the way.'

There's a long and painful silence as they look at me and wait. I know I mustn't let them take the car, but I don't know how to tell them. There is a chance my mother wouldn't notice that the car was missing. She doesn't go out on Wednesdays and, if she did realize it was gone and the keys weren't there, she'd probably assume that Dad had come home for the car because he needed it at work. He has been known to do that.

'Look,' I start to explain. I know I mustn't get pushed into something that I'm only going to regret. 'If my dad found out, he'd go berserk. If he knew I had anything to do with it, he'd kill me.'

There's another unpleasant silence. 'Your father wouldn't kill you.' Ralph looks at me directly. 'You know that's an exaggeration.'

I suppose it is, but he must understand what I mean.

'The bloody world's about to be blown up,' he tells me. 'And what we're doing might stop it. It's the history of civilization that's at stake—what the hell does it matter if you get a bit of hassle from your dad when you get back home?'

I hadn't thought of it like that and, when I do, I realize that what Ralph says is true. Helping D.A.M.N. achieve their objectives—helping them to storm the missile base is the most important thing I've done in my life so far. Getting rid of the nuclear missiles is probably the most essential thing that's ever been done in human history. In comparison with that, getting told off by my dad is completely insignificant. I feel ashamed that I ever thought of it as important.

Julie squeezes me round the waist and snuggles up to me closely. 'Can you really drive, Chris?' she asks me.

'Of course I can drive.'

'Go on, then. Go and fetch the car.'

I give her a squeeze in return. 'O.K.' I nod my head. 'Are you coming with me, Trev?'

16

I can't count the number of times I've walked up Hagg Farm Lane feeling completely alienated from the middle-class world of sun-deck patios and polystyrene Greek urns. This morning I still feel separate, but I don't feel like an outcast. I feel that what I'm doing is important, much more essential than knitting and polishing cars and shopping at the supermarket. I can see further than anyone else. I have a mission to fulfil, an essential role to play in the survival of the world. Like Ralph said, all the petty hassles and trivia just don't matter any more. I know that what I'm doing is right. For the first time in my life I feel completely free.

I'd prefer it if Trevor didn't have to see the garden full of gnomes, but I tell myself that doesn't matter either—not when the future of the world is at stake. 'We grow gnomes in our garden,' I tell him confidently as we turn to walk up the drive. 'Other people grow grass and flowers and stuff, but we grow gnomes.'

Trevor stares at the garden in amazement. His mouth opens and closes soundlessly. He shakes his head. 'We grow dog muck in ours,' he says at last.

We walk round the corner past Wishful Willy gazing into his wishing-well. 'You'd better watch that gnome when you back the car out,' I explain to Trevor. 'He sticks out a bit.'

'O.K.'

Trevor sees the car and stops and whistles under his breath. 'Is that it?' he asks.

'That's it.'

'Not bad.'

'If you wait under the carport,' I tell him, 'I'll pass the keys out through that little window.'

'O.K.'

There are two windows opening on to the carport: one from the downstairs toilet and the other from the kitchen. I'm assuming that he'll have the sense to keep out of sight from the kitchen.

I open the front door quietly and tiptoe into the hall. On the wall is a wooden elephant with a knot in its tail and a notice saying, *Don't forget your keys*. I unhook the car keys from the elephant's trunk and take them into the loo. I daren't just drop them through the window because of the grate outside. I climb on the bog and poke my head through the toilet window.

'*Pssssst.*'

Trevor's still gawping at the monogrammed mudflaps, the laminated sunhatch and the wash/wipers on the headlamps. He's standing in front of the kitchen window with his hand in the air, presumably waiting for my mother to hand him the keys as she finishes the washing-up.

'*Pssssst.*'

He sees me at last and slides towards me with his back to the wall, like a secret agent in a spy film. I hope my mother hasn't seen him. I pass out the keys, climb off the bog, then stroll into the kitchen to keep my mother's attention distracted whilst Trevor nicks the car.

My mother's polishing the teapot. 'What are you doing home?' she asks me.

'I'd forgotten that school's not starting till late today,' I tell her. 'The teachers are having their annual general meeting.'

'Oh.'

There are several advantages in having a mother who's as thick as a short-legged coffee table. One is that making up fabrications requires the minimum of brain power.

'I'd forgotten that we're doing Cookery on Wednesdays now,' I explain, 'so I thought I could nip back home for the ingredients.' I want my mum to climb up to the top shelf in the cupboard so that she'll have her back to the kitchen window. The cupboard door is open, so I start making a mental list of all the ingredients I can see up there.

'But what about Metalwork? I always have to have your craft apron ironed for Wednesdays.'

'Miss Salt had a nervous breakdown, so the Metalwork teacher's doing Cookery with us instead.'

My mother looks hopelessly confused. 'But I haven't starched your apron yet . . .'

Trevor should be in the car by now. I must get her over

to the cupboard quickly. 'It doesn't matter about the apron,' I tell her. 'I'll use the Metalwork one for Cookery. I need some angelica and . . .'

'Do you want your Cookery apron starching for Metalwork, then?'

'It doesn't matter.' I find myself almost shouting at her. 'Look, I've got to hurry up now. I need some angelica and some dried peas, dehydrated onion rings, sultanas, yeast, birthday candles . . .'

'Just a minute. I'll have a look in the cupboard.'

Trevor's massive face looms up at the window just as my mother turns towards the cupboard. She's missed him by a fraction of a second. I can't understand why he isn't in the car yet.

My mother climbs up the step-ladder stool to look in the cupboard. 'Well, I think we've got most of those,' she mutters. 'The sultanas *were* for the Christmas cake, but I can get some more.'

My mother starts organizing Christmas as soon as we get back from our summer holidays. 'What are you making, then?'

Out of the corner of my eye, I can see the top of the car slowly gliding past the kitchen window. I hope Trevor doesn't go into the wall. Our drive isn't very wide.

'Sorry?'

'What are you making with all these different ingredients?'

I should have worked that out. I struggle hard to think of a recipe that could use all the ingredients from the top shelf of my mother's cupboard. I can't even remember now what I've asked her to get. 'Curry.'

'Curry? With birthday candles?'

'It's a special kind of birthday curry. It's an ancient Pakistani custom . . .'

'Well, I've never heard of that before.'

'It's all part of this ethnic cookery course we're doing.'

Suddenly, the car engine starts up. I don't know what Trevor thinks he's doing. He should have been able to back the car out of the drive without needing to switch the engine on. I have to drown out the noise. I stamp across to the sink and turn both taps on full, then I start singing and drop the teapot on the floor.

'What *are* you doing, Christopher?'

'Just washing my hands.'

The engine on the car is very quiet. There's quite a good chance my mum won't notice it. I pick up the teapot and then start washing my hands, still singing and clattering the occasional fork and teaspoon.

'You're making a lot of noise.'

There's a crash from outside. It sounds as if Wishful Willy's bitten the dust. Oh no. I switch the radio on. I'll have to leave as soon as I can and go and inspect the damage.

'We don't want the wireless on at this time of the morning.'

'I just want to check the time.' I wish she'd hurry up. I'll have to go and rescue Willy, because he sits in full view of the living-room window. My mum might not notice the vanished car, but there's no way she could sit in the house all day and ignore a splattered garden gnome.

My mum walks down the step-ladder with an armful of ingredients. 'I don't know what you're going to do with all this yeast . . .'

'It's to make the curry rise,' I tell her, grabbing the packets out of her hand and ramming them into a plastic bag. 'I'll have to be going now. It's later than I thought.'

'Will you be having this curry at school, then? Because I don't think your dad'll want it for his tea.'

'Yes. Like I said, it's a special birthday ceremony, so I'll be home a bit late. I'll be playing chess as well.'

'All right. I'll put your dinner in the oven if you're not back.'

'Thanks.' I grab the plastic carrier and dive towards the front door.

Trevor's backed the car down on to the street, but the damage to the gnome is worse than I expected. Willy's been sliced apart at the knees and his corpse is slowly rolling down the path. I rush after him and pick him up and then try to balance his body on the little stumps of legs left by the wishing-well. He just falls over. I can't think what else to do with him, so I ram his legless body in with the birthday curry stuff and dash out on to the street.

Trevor's got every possible gadget working on the car. The hazard-warning lights are flashing; the electric windows are whirring up and down; the sunhatch in the roof is slowly opening and closing; the wash/wipers are dancing away on the headlights and the rear window and it isn't even raining.

Trev opens the door for me. I leap into the car with my gnome and collapse with a sigh of relief against the caviar-cloth seat trim. Trev stamps his foot down on the accelerator and we're off. I can hardly believe it's worked.

The dashboard on a San Marino is like a control panel in a spaceship. Trevor tries out all the different knobs and switches as he drives. The ashtray-overspill hazard-warning is bleeping away already. The remote-control passenger door mirror is whirling backwards and forwards and the fingertip-control push-button stereo is resounding with Vera Lynn singing 'There'll always be an England'.

'You're driving too fast,' I warn Trevor. We're doing thirty-three miles an hour in a built-up area.

'You can drive if you want to, when we've picked the others up.'

I push the lever on my seat into the full reclining position. I think it's safest for me to remain invisible as we coast down Hagg Farm Lane.

Trev looks round in amazement at my boots waving in the air. 'I wondered where you'd gone,' he says, grinning. 'I thought I must have pressed the ejector-seat button by mistake.'

I sit upright again as we round the corner by the chip shop. The others are standing waiting and the Mini-van is out of sight.

Trevor gets out of the car and I move over into the driver's seat as everyone else climbs in. I switch off the wipers and the hazard-warning lights and everything else we don't need and turn Vera Lynn down to half-volume. Julie opens the front passenger door and gawps at Wishful Willy lying legless on the front seat. 'What's that?' she exclaims.

'A garden gnome. Pass it back to Ralph. He can put it on the rear parcel shelf.'

I'm pleased Julie's sitting in the front because I'd like to impress her with my driving. I haven't had many lessons yet, but I've studied the Highway Code and pride myself on being a careful and considerate driver.

'The rendezvous is at 1100 hours,' says Ralph. 'That gives us seventy-three minutes and fifteen seconds . . .'

I go through my checklist process: handbrake, gear lever, mirror, whirr down the window and look behind me . . .

'Haven't you got any better tapes?' moans Julie.

I reach across to the in-car entertainment library. 'The titles are in there,' I tell her.

When I've waited for the traffic coming past, I edge

forward carefully into the road, keeping my hands positioned at exactly 1500 hours on the hand-knitted steering-wheel glove. I drive into the flow of traffic then glance across at Julie to see if she's impressed.

Julie hasn't looked up. She's still skimming scornfully through the cassetologue. 'We've got *The Gay Gordons and other Olde Tyme Favourites*,' she sneers. '*Selections from Famous Military Balls* . . .'

Everybody howls with laughter.

'The full soundtrack of *Trooping the Colour* played by the Coldstream Guards . . . *Max Bygraves' Greatest Hits, Volume 27* . . .'

On the horizon, there's a pedestrian crossing, so I start to go through my gear changes: from fourth to third, across the H and down into second, then, manipulating the monogrammed, knitted gear-stick cover deftly in the palm of my hand, I ease forward into first . . .

'And what's this? *Tunes from Trumpton*. Oh no, look at this: *Children's Favourites—with love to Christopher from Mummy and Daddy*. "Nelly the Elephant", "I'm a Pink Toothbrush, you're a Blue Toothbrush". . .'

I cringe with embarrassment as I stop the car at the pedestrian crossing, beckoning politely to a little old lady to let her know it's safe to cross. She just smiles at me and shakes her head. I think she's only stopped for a moment whilst her dog cocks its leg against a lamp-post. I go into neutral and put the handbrake on, while I look carefully left and right to see if anyone else is waiting to cross the road.

'Have we run out of petrol or what?' asks Mike.

I try not to let myself get agitated as I set off once again. Julie's now sitting with her feet up on the top of the glove compartment. I wish she'd taken her boots off first. She keeps trying out the different tapes then takes them off after only a couple of bars. Some of the comments she makes about 'Nelly the Elephant', *Trumpton* and the *Famous Military Balls* are unrepeatable.

I drive along smoothly at a steady twenty-five miles an hour. 'Can't you get a move on, Chris?' says Ralph. 'We've only forty-eight minutes before we're due to rendezvous at grid reference 860908.'

Anyone can tell that we're still in a built-up area. I increase the speed reluctantly to twenty-nine miles an hour.

As we drive out of the town centre, we get stuck behind a lorry load of frozen fish. 'Why can't we overtake it?' asks Mike.

'We're approaching the brow of a hill.'

'Oh yes,' scoffs Trevor. 'With a gradient of one in thirty-nine.'

I try to maintain an accurate distance of eighty metres behind the fish lorry as it travels over the hill and round a bend.

'Why can't we overtake it now?'

'There's an unbroken white line in the centre of the road.'

'On the other side,' says Trevor.

I wish they wouldn't keep harassing me, and I wish that Julie wouldn't drop her cigarette ash on the carpet.

'Right,' says Mike. 'We're on an open stretch of road with not a hill or a bend in sight. Could anybody tell me why we can't overtake the fish lorry?'

'We're not going bloody fast enough,' Julie scoffs.

We arrive on the outskirts of Bedgar forty-nine minutes late and find a cordon of police cars and barriers.

'Come on, Chris,' urges Mike. 'Just crash through. We can easy knock 'em flying!'

I've seen dozens of films of car chases where drivers crash their way through barriers and send police cars spinning upside down and policemen leaping frantically for cover. But I don't fancy trying that in my father's G. T. San Marino. I pull in carefully to the side of the road and go into neutral, then I pull on the handbrake and whirr down the window as a policeman strides towards us.

He pokes his head inside the car. 'Can you tell me what your business is in Bedgar?' he asks, frowning quizzically at the dismembered corpse of Wishful Willy on the rear parcel shelf.

'We've come for a picnic,' offers Ralph at last. 'We'd heard there are some nice beauty spots round here.'

The policeman doesn't look impressed. 'Do you have any evidence to support that?' he asks.

Ralph looks at us helplessly. Then I remember my lunch. I search around for the sandwich bag and see it poking out from underneath Trevor on the back seat. 'Yes!' I yell enthusiastically, as I tug it out. 'Here you are!' I pass the plastic bag across with a superior grin.

The policeman opens up the bag suspiciously, then pulls out between his thumb and forefinger a compressed wadge of cold fried egg plastered together with peanut butter and shreds of soggy toast. He stares at it as if it's the fossilized remains of a rare species of mammoth dung. 'What's this?' he asks.

'Egg yukky,' I tell him. 'Do you want to try some? We always take some with us on a picnic.'

I think about showing him the ingredients of the birthday curry as well, but decide against it. Even my mother had her doubts about that.

The fuzz won't sample the egg yukky and he won't let us go to the U.S. base to have our picnic either. He makes us turn the car round which isn't easy, as I've only done

U-turns so far and the road isn't very wide. I wish my father had a smaller car. I finish up having to drive a few metres on the pavement, scraping the car against a bramble bush and narrowly missing a tree. Then we set off to find a different route to the base.

17

We try another route, but there are road blocks there as well, so we turn around and drive into Bedgar village —which doesn't consist of much except a street full of shops, a village church and a pub. It's the pub that makes us decide to park the car and look around. There are quite a few groups of D.A.M.N. supporters, strolling about, wearing badges and carrying placards. Old-age pensioners and country housewives stare as if they've just been invaded by a new species from a distant planet.

We walk inside the pub called, believe it or not, The Gay Farmer and buy a round of drinks. There's a smattering of country yokels in there . . . or perhaps they're all gay farmers, I'm not sure . . . but none of them speak to us. Most of the other D.A.M.N. supporters find their way to the pub eventually. I feel a bit embarrassed about walking in there with my carrier-bag and Wishful Willy tucked under my arm, but Ralph insists that we remove all evidence from the car.

I hide Wishful Willy under the table and we sit around boozing, doodling *Gay Farmers against the Bomb* on the beer mats and arguing tactics for smashing our way through police cordons. It seems a fairly futile discussion because I don't think we've more than eight or nine cars and vans between us plus about fifty supporters. The idea of the secret campaign is a dead loss because the police have obviously sussed it all out.

By the time we've downed a few drinks, there's a growing spirit of bravado in the pub. People say that the police won't still be waiting for us—that they'll have gone off duty by now—and, if we drive out to the base together in a convoy, and get there before we're spotted by helicopters, early-warning satellites, or whatever, then there's nothing much that we can't do.

The optimism is infectious—or perhaps it's just that we're all tanked up—but, an hour or so later, we walk out of the pub several centimetres taller than we went in, shouting slogans, clenching our fists in the air and generally raring to go. Outside, the shouting suddenly stops as we stand and stare at the scene in front of us. It's incredible. Like something out of a film set.

Down at the other end of the street is an absolute army of policemen. They aren't just standing round in groups, chattering and admiring the scenery: they're lined up rank by rank in battle formation, carrying riot shields, like toy soldiers in a model kit. You almost expect to see unneatened edges—thin, frayed bits of plastic that fastened them to the mould as they were stamped out in the factory. They start to slowly stride towards us down the street.

I look around to see who the cops are after, expecting to find another rival army closing in behind us. There's no one there. The crowds of shoppers and the traffic have mysteriously vanished. The street in front of us has emptied. We're left exposed and isolated as the palisade of policemen continues to edge towards us.

All the carefully planned schedules haven't prepared us for this so no one knows what to do. It seems so incredible—if we'd done something illegal you could understand the fuzz appearing in full force, but we've done nothing to upset them yet.

The riot shields are lined up like targets, waiting to have things thrown at them. Someone yells: 'Come on. Spread out!' Then there's a confused noise of shouting. 'Get something to chuck at them!' 'Grab the bottles!'

Hands reach out and snatch empty bottles and glasses from the wall and tables outside the pub; people pick up wooden stools; a few blokes wrestle with the parasols planted in the centre of the tables and then we spread right out across the street, brandishing weapons and fists and hurling abuse against the fuzz.

I don't pick up a bottle or anything because, by the time I think about turning round and grabbing one, the wall and tables are empty. I just cling on tightly to Wishful Willy as I get sandwiched between the rest of the mob and we set off down the street. I realize that I've managed to leave my carrier-bag behind me in the pub, but when I turn round I notice that the doors have suddenly closed.

We start to move forward. The police stop dead. A single bottle skims through the air and smashes in front of the riot shields. It's followed by an array of missiles: empty beer cans clatter against metallic shields; ashtrays whizz across and bounce off helmets; Trevor lobs a bar stool through the air as if it's a plastic Frisbee and the whole police rank breaks into disarray as they start to retreat, stumbling backwards over each other's feet.

A great cheer goes up from our side and we start to move further forward, spreading out and scouring the street for anything that can be thrown. A litter-bin is unhooked and sent spinning through the air, spilling out screwed-up chip papers and raining cigarette-ends down on the fuzz. More bottles whizz through the air, and the air is heavy with the shattering of glass. The police are near enough to see the expressions on their faces. They look afraid and stupid, as if they weren't expecting us to react like this. I begin to think that defeating them will be easy.

There's nothing else left in the road that we can throw —not without digging up the paving-stones. The shops on either side are all locked up with their shutters pulled down tightly. All except the pet shop. Right in the middle of the row there's a shop called *Hatcher's Garden Centre and Pet Emporium*. Halfway down the plate-glass window is a notice saying, *Ornamental rocks—half price*. Everybody piles in.

Inside the window is a mountain of ornamental rocks. The shop assistants have disappeared and, within twenty seconds, so have all the rocks. People stagger out of the shop doorway, bent half double with arms full of boulders. When there are no more rocks, they grab bags of dog biscuits, tins of flea powder and boxes of cat litter.

It's only a few minutes before the pet shop has been stripped bare of everything except the animals, their cages and some fish. Then a woman puts a hamster cage on the floor, tips out the contents and scurries out of the door holding the empty cage and yelling, 'Animal Liberation!'

The animal liberation slogan really catches on and within a couple of minutes there are animals everywhere, as people tip tortoises and gerbils, snakes and budgerigars out of their cages. The pet shop floor becomes a seething carpet of furry mammals, crawling reptiles and the occasional gasping fish. As a brightly coloured snake slithers towards me, I decide it's time to go.

Back in the street, the riot's in full swing. I thread my way across to Julie, who's busy skimming tins of flea powder down towards the riot shields. 'Come on,' she says, pointing to a gap in the riot shields. 'Lob something over there!'

At last I've found a constructive use for one of my father's garden gnomes. I walk back a few paces then take a run, remembering what I've learned at school in javelin practice. I thrust the whole weight of my body behind Wishful Willy as I launch him into the air, leaping forward with the momentum. I feel a sense of freedom, of power and release as I watch Willy flying beautifully high, his pointed cap spinning as he soars. I will the gnome to die, to splatter into a thousand tiny fragments as he reaches a peak and then plummets, nose-diving wonkily towards the street.

Wishful Willy splashes down on the tarmac, bounces on his backside, wobbles a bit, then settles horizontally in the middle of the riot. He looks at me reproachfully. I think I've flattened his nose and knocked the end off his fishing-rod, but, apart from that, he looks much the same as he did before.

'Super tough gnome,' remarks Julie.

I nod my head in resignation.

The street is in absolute chaos. A policeman's lying injured on the ground and, when others go to help him, they get pelted with a whole barrage of missiles. He looks as if he's unconscious. There are sirens blaring out as more police arrive with reinforcements; I notice a youth with blood streaming from his face being led away to an ambulance.

I dodge through flying missiles, keeping an eye on the police, who are re-grouping rapidly. Suddenly, I see a large gun barrel pointing over one of the riot shields. The implications don't register at first. Then I hear a shot and something whistles past me overhead. The next thing I know is that there's smoke—a cloud of it appearing on my right. People start running away in all directions, coughing and spluttering with hands across their eyes. 'Tear gas!' The word spreads through the crowd. There's another heavy shot and everybody scatters.

'Come on, Chris!' I hear Julie yelling. 'Get out of the way!' I run to the side of the street.

The clouds of gas distort my view. All I get are impressions—isolated incidents. A woman runs past me, sobbing, with her hand across her eyes and blood streaming down her arm. A few blokes dive into the cloud of gas and drag out a youth, about my age, who's lying on the roadway, coughing and spluttering. Another youth is being carried on a stretcher to an ambulance. Then, to the right of me, there's a scuffle.

A policeman is holding Ralph by the arm and trying to lead him away, while Mike and Trevor are dragging him back. The policeman gives up, lets go of Ralph and turns to walk away.

Trevor lunges forward and brings the policeman crashing to the ground. I can hear the crack as his head smashes against the kerb. The policeman is lying helpless, almost hidden from view by the bodies of Mike, Ralph and Trevor and by the drifting clouds of gas. His helmet has been knocked off in the fall and, from where I stand, I can see blood oozing from his mouth. His left arm is sticking out from underneath him, disjointed and out of shape like the leg of a frog. Mike kicks the policeman's injured arm. He howls in pain, cowering in the roadway, sobbing.

I stand motionless and stare as Mike, Trevor and Ralph take turns in kicking at the policeman's body. With every blow he shudders and cries out. He raises his right arm to ward off the blows, but Mike grabs hold of his wrist and holds it steady in the air to make space for the boots to kick and trample, thudding into his body. I stand transfixed.

The policeman is crying out loud for them to stop. He tries to curl up his body to protect himself, but Mike seizes his broken arm from underneath him and yanks it fiercely upwards, forcing the blue uniform into a straightened line for the kicks to hammer home. I catch a glimpse of the policeman's face—swollen, red and bleeding—before Mike smashes into it with his boot.

Ralph and Trevor have their heads down, aiming blows with precision, but Mike's face is clearly visible. His eyes are gloating. He looks elated, glowing with fervour and delight. Suddenly, I hate him.

A gang of policemen arrive from nowhere. Mike and Trevor see them first and they turn and run. Ralph's reaction is slower. He's still kicking the injured policeman on the ground when the others grab him from behind and twist his arms behind his back. Ralph swears at them and struggles as they frog-march him away.

There's another shot of tear gas and another cloud erupts in front of me. 'Come on, Chris,' I hear Trev yelling. 'Get a move on! Get back to the car!'

I stumble after them through the cloud of gas, trying to keep my eyes screwed tightly closed. I spread out my arms in front of me, but soon find my way blocked by a confusion of bodies, lamp-posts and walls. I have to keep opening my eyes and, when I do, the stinging is unbearable as if they've been bandaged with raw onion. The others have run ahead of me; they don't wait for me or come back to see if I'm all right. They leave me to stumble onwards, completely blinded now and crying, the tears swilling down my cheeks. I lose all sense of direction, turning down unknown side-streets—anywhere to get away from the clouds of gas. At last I hear them shouting at me. 'Chris! Over here!'

I stagger onwards in the direction of the noise. I hear the sound of a car pulling up beside me. A door opens; an arm grabs hold of me and forces me on to a seat. The door closes and the car sets off.

18

We're in such a hurry to get out of Bedgar village that we take the wrong turning and finish up lost, way out in the countryside. Trevor pushes the road atlas into my hand and expects me to navigate, but my eyes are still stinging too much to try and focus and the map is just a blur. 'Change places with Mike,' Trevor tells me. 'He can find the route if he's sitting in the front.'

We stop the car for a minute while Mike and I change places. I collapse on the back seat next to Julie; all I want to do is rest and recover. I feel weary and sickened, wanting to be alone, to sort out in my mind what I feel about D.A.M.N. and the riot. I'm worried as well about what's going to happen when my father finds out about the car.

The others are elated. 'It was fantastic, wasn't it?' Julie says, wrapping her arm around me. I nod my head in resignation.

'Yeah,' says Trevor. 'We got rid of a few coppers as well.'

Mike laughs. 'That pig we worked over won't be on duty again this year.'

'Serves him right. He should have left Ralph alone.'

'He'll know better next time, anyhow.'

I close my eyes and I see the policeman lying injured in the gutter, his body writhing in pain.

I feel sick.

Julie has one arm around my waist; her other hand is deftly stroking the inside of my thigh. I wish she'd leave me alone. My mind is in a state of turmoil and I want to sit alone and think things out. Julie's just distracting me. 'Let's have the radio on,' she says to Mike. 'There might be something about it on the news.'

Mike switches the radio to the local station, and we listen to record requests for the inhabitants of Bedgar and thereabouts. People request records for their grand-parents, their next-door neighbours, dogs and cats and husbands at work. I wish they wouldn't. I remember something Sarah said to me about policemen only being ordinary men inside uniforms, and I think about the policeman lying injured on the road as having a wife and kids and maybe a dog, the sort of ordinary bloke people request records for on the radio. The thought frightens me.

I can't remember exactly what Sarah said—something about how you can't attack a uniform without harming the man inside it, and I think about Mike's face gloating with pleasure as he thrust the weight of his boot into the policeman's face. I realize with a flash of insight that that's what wars are made of—people attacking uniforms and ignoring the fact that inside them are ordinary people like themselves.

Julie's hand is now stroking uncomfortably high on my thigh. I wish she'd stop. I don't like to move her hand away, but I don't know how to distract her. I turn my face to her and kiss her lightly on the cheek. She moves her mouth around until it reaches mine and then starts to kiss me passionately, working her tongue around my lips and my teeth and then the inside of my mouth. I still feel sick. Thankfully, the news comes on the radio.

'Thirteen policemen were injured today after being called in to suppress a riot in Bedgar village,' the newsreader starts off. 'Observers reported that demonstrators, who were unable to reach the nearby military base, ran completely amok, causing damage estimated at many thousands of pounds. Police were forced to use tear gas to dispel the rioting youths and more than twenty-five arrests were made.'

'*Police called in to suppress a riot!*' Mike scoffs. 'It was them that bloody started it!'

'And what about us getting hurt?' adds Julie. 'We could all have been blinded by that tear gas!'

'Bevan Barnforth, Member of Parliament for the nearby Ryecroft constituency, himself an active campaigner in the local peace movement, was asked to comment about the riot . . .'

'Oh, my God!' shrieks Julie. 'Not him. Spare us . . .'

It seems odd to hear Bevan Barnforth speaking on the radio after I've talked with him in his living-room. 'All those of us who are active in the peace movement,' he starts off, 'want to make it clear that we give no support whatsoever to groups like this. We never condone this kind of action and I can only extend my sympathy to those policemen who have been injured and to their families . . .'

'But you have been known to campaign yourself for Direct Action . . .' the reporter interrupts.

'For Non-Violent Direct Action, yes. Some of our members joined a peace camp outside one of the missile bases and several were arrested, but none were involved in acts of violence. Violence goes against everything that we're working for. The peace movement has to be peaceful . . .'

'Oh, get him off!' says Mike. 'We've heard enough.'

'I bet he turns up at the next meeting, anyway,' says Trevor. 'Him or that bloody Sarah.'

'We'll have that Animal Lovers against the Bomb mob to contend with as well,' adds Julie. 'They'll be moaning all night about how many goldfish got annihilated!'

Mike switches off the radio and we lean back in our seats. Julie starts kissing me again. Her left arm is squeezing round my waist, which isn't doing my heaving stomach any good, and her right hand is feverishly working its way round my crotch. I just can't take it any more. I push her away.

'What's the matter?' she asks, obviously offended.

'I'm not feeling too good,' I tell her. 'I think it's the tear gas.' I shuffle into the corner of the seat, lean my head on my arm and close my eyes.

We've found the right road now away from Bedgar and Trev has his foot firmly down on the accelerator. I dread to think what speed we're doing, but if there's still a chance of getting home before my dad comes back from work, I suppose we ought to take it. We haven't planned anything about how we're going to get the car back. I wish Ralph was here. He'd have organized it properly. I was assuming that the others would clean the car up, take it and park it under the carport, and all I'd have to do was walk nonchalantly up the road, planning out stories about the birthday curry and the chess match, but I can't see it happening now. I look at my watch. Thirty-five minutes to go before my dad gets home. I have a premonition of disaster.

I try to recapture the realization that I had this morning, that cars and hassles with parents aren't of any importance whatsoever when the future of the world is at stake. But the elation is gone. I do know that the peace movement is more important than my father's car, but I also know that what we've done today is wrong. Peaceful marches haven't been successful in stopping the missiles, but at least they haven't put people against us. All that Sarah said to me about gaining public support and sympathy starts to make sense. When I get the chance, I'd like to talk to her about it. I think maybe now I could agree with her much more than I agree with D.A.M.N.

I open my eyes and look out of the window as we overtake a white car. 'That's the police, you fool,' Mike says to Trev. 'You don't overtake cop cars at ninety miles an hour!'

'Well, if we're breaking the speed limit, so are they,' says Trev. 'They must be doing eighty at least.'

We haven't put any petrol in the car. Ralph did say we'd fill it up before we took it back, but there won't be time for that now. I press the button again on my watch. Fifteen minutes to go. We might just make it.

I close my eyes again and find myself starting to doze. There are so many things I need to sort out in my mind. I can't work out what to say when I get back home because I don't know whether they'll have realized that the car's been missing. I've had very little sleep this week through getting up early to wait for my telephone call so, as my eyes close, I find myself drifting into a hazy dream of heavy boots and policemen, and the plodding of my father's footsteps as he paces up and down the carport looking for his car.

Suddenly, we swerve. I open my eyes with a jolt as I realize that there's something wrong. 'Bloody hell!' shouts Mike.

Through the windscreen I can see a huge tanker heading straight towards us. We're on the wrong side of the road. To the left of us is a motorbike. It takes only a second for the scene to register. Trevor's been overtaking the motorbike whilst approaching the brow of a hill. The tanker's now crashing down towards us. If we swerve any more we could hit the motorbike; if we stay as we are, we'll be splattered.

Trevor wrenches round the steering-wheel. There's a screech of brakes. The outside world flashes past: I see a close-up of the tanker, of a tree, the road . . . the motorbike . . . then everything blurs into one. Julie gasps. The car tilts upwards; we're driving on two wheels and the world is lop-sided like the view from a landing aircraft. Then the car rights itself. We swerve again. There's a horrendous thud on Trevor's side of the car, and I find myself being flung forward against Mike's seat. I put up my hands to my face. Then there's an explosion, a frightening bang as if someone's shot at us. The car stops dead and I thud backwards in my seat with Julie thrown beside me. My head rocks back with the momentum. I close my eyes again and wait for death.

19

A sequence of my life's main events is supposed to flash through my thoughts like a newsreel. It doesn't happen. My mind is a blank, an emptiness. There's a pause whilst I struggle to bring myself back to reality. I need to find out whether I'm alive or not. I think I am. I open my eyes. Slowly, the world around me creeps back into focus. I'm still in the car. Julie is lying beside me. Trevor's collapsed with his head down on the steering-wheel and Mike is sitting next to him. The world is silent. There's a hole in the top corner of the windscreen and the rest of the glass is a frosted mosaic pattern. It was like that in the winter when the windows were covered with ice.

'Is everybody O.K.?' asks Mike.

It's a while before anyone answers. 'I'm all right,' I say at last. I think I am. Most of me seems to be still in place. My neck hurts, but I don't think it's actually broken. My head's still here on top of it, anyway.

Julie raises her head. 'I'm O.K.,' she mutters.

Trevor's still slumped against the steering-wheel. 'You all right, Trev?' asks Mike.

Trevor nods slowly. 'Did we miss the bike?' he asks.

'I think so. I'll have a look in a minute.' Mike reaches for the door handle, but makes no attempt at opening the door.

'I thought we'd had it with that tanker,' says Julie. 'It was coming straight for us.'

'You did some damn good driving there, mate,' Mike says, placing his hand on Trevor's shoulder. 'We could all have been done for.'

I don't know how he dares to say that about Trevor's driving. I open my mouth to object, then change my mind. There isn't much point.

'We'd better have a look at what's happened, then,' says Mike.

He climbs out of the car. I ought to get out as well, but I can't bring myself to look at the damage to the car or the squashed motorcyclist. I lie back for a few seconds and do nothing.

'The bike's not here,' calls Mike. 'It's gone!'

I force myself to clamber out of the car and walk around it. We've crashed into a tree. The whole of the front of the car is buckled. The lights are smashed, the front bumper is hanging on by a thread and the driver's door has just about caved in. Trevor climbs out through the other door, and we stand and stare at the damage.

'It's not too bad, is it?' says Trevor. 'I thought it would be a write-off.'

The tanker has pulled up further down on the other side of the road. The driver climbs out of his cab. He scowls at us angrily. He looks as though he's about to cross over and have a row with us, but then he seems to change his mind. He shakes his head in exasperation, then climbs back into his cab and drives away.

Julie gets out of the car and comes and puts her arm on my shoulder. We've got to do something with the car. I don't know what, but we can't just stand around staring at it. I gaze at the broken glass from the headlights, lying scattered in the mud and I think of the Sundays my dad has spent polishing his car.

I don't want him to see it like this. I can see our estate just over the brow of the hill. I could walk back in fifteen or twenty minutes, but I don't know what to do about the car. If the police were to find us walking away from it, they'd certainly take us in. I start to panic. My legs are still weak and jellified from the effects of the crash. I feel shocked and frightened. I feel like crying.

'Remember that police car we passed?' says Mike. 'I bet they'll be coming this way.'

We're on a country road with no buses. We might be able to thumb a lift, but there's hardly any traffic. And if the police pick me up near where my father's car has just crashed . . .

We're near the top of the hill and by the side of the road is a steep drop. It's obvious what we've got to do. 'Let's shove the car down there,' I suggest, pointing to the dried-up stream way down in the valley.

'*What?*'

'We'll have to get it out of the way. If the cops drive up and see us hanging around, we've had it. If we shove the car down there it might be weeks before they find it.'

Mike looks at me incredulously. 'But, we'd wreck it . . .' he objects.

I gaze at the remains of the laminated windscreen and the bashed-up front. 'It's wrecked already.'

'No, it's not,' says Trev. 'All it needs are a couple of new panels, two new doors, a bumper and lights and stuff. It's still a decent car.'

'It could do with a re-spray,' adds Mike, glancing at the huge scars made by the tree in the rear metallic paintwork.

I start to get more agitated. We've got to shift the car out of the way before the police come past. 'Come on,' I urge them. 'We could easily shove it.'

'You're not talking sense,' says Trevor. 'Your dad could have the car mended. It won't cost him much . . .'

'Once we crash it down there, it'll be a write-off,' Mike explains.

If the police were to tow the San Marino up the drive like this, it would just about kill my father. The kindest thing would be to ensure that he never set eyes on it again. 'We've got to get rid of it,' I insist. 'The cops'll be here soon.'

'It's Chris that's got to decide,' says Julie. 'It's his dad's car and he's the one that'll get the blame.'

Mike shakes his head at me in despair. 'Well, it's your decision, Chris. You're going to have to take the responsibility . . .'

'We'll need to back it off the tree first. We might have to shove it from the front.' I just want to be doing something.

'All we've done is dented it a bit,' argues Trevor. 'You can't make us responsible for wrecking it.'

I want to scream at them. It doesn't matter whose responsibility it is. We've just got to get it out of the way.

'We'll see whether we can move it first,' says Trevor. He climbs into the driver's seat, puts the gear into reverse. The wheels whirr round a bit, but the car stays still.

The rest of us stand by the tree and shove. The car eases backwards slightly. Then Trevor turns the wheel smoothly round so the car is facing down the embankment. He pulls on the handbrake, then turns and looks at Mike.

'Let's get this straight, Chris,' says Mike. 'This car is your responsibility. If you ask us to give it a shove, we will do. But, as far as we're concerned, you were driving the car when it swerved into a tree and down the embankment and you leapt out before it crashed. O.K.?'

I don't see that it matters. 'That's O.K.'

'So, would you like us to shove the car?'

Of course I want them to shove the bloody car. 'Yes!' I yell.

'Ask us, then.'

I take a deep breath to stop myself from screaming. 'Please will you help me to shove the bloody car?'

'O.K., Trev?'

'O.K.' They don't even bother asking Julie what she thinks.

Trevor climbs out and walks round to the back of the car.

'You get in the driver's seat, Chris,' says Mike, 'and take the keys out. You'll have to steer it a bit, then jump out as soon as it gets going.'

'O.K.' I climb into the driver's seat. I have to move the seat right forward because my legs are so much shorter than Trevor's. I take out the keys and put them in my pocket. There are a few trees and rocks ahead. I have to steer the car round those. After that there's just a drop. If

I'm still in the car when it goes down there, I'll be dead.

I squint at the windscreen and try to make out where the trees and rocks are. I can't see anything. 'We'll have to smash the windscreen,' I tell them. 'I'll have to see out.'

I clamber out of the car again. Trevor grabs a stone and smashes the windscreen from inside. Most of the glass lands on the bonnet, but a lot of it goes inside—on the front hockey-stick armrests, the illuminated front ashtray and on the seat where I have to sit. Trevor takes the duster out of the glove compartment and begins to wipe away the glass. I take a deep breath. I'd like to smoke a cigarette, but there's no time. I realize that I'm sweating. I take off my jacket and pass it to Julie. 'Look after this for me, will you?' I ask her.

'O.K., then, Chris?' says Trevor.

I look down at the driver's seat which is still speckled with broken glass. I take off my sweater and lay it across the seat. It's quite a cool day, but I'm sweating so much it doesn't matter.

I take a last deep breath and then climb into the car. I place my hands on my mother's hand-knitted steering-wheel glove. Then I take off the brake. I mustn't jump out too soon. If I leave the car before it's passed the rocks and trees, then it'll just bump into something; it won't even reach the drop. I mustn't chicken out by jumping too quickly.

I reach up and adjust the rear-view mirror until it's filled by a close-up of Trevor's face. I notice the muscles on his face begin to tighten as he starts to shove the car.

The car moves forward. I want to shout that I'm not ready. I haven't got myself psyched up yet, but it's too late now. I'm off.

The car rolls faster than I expected. The ground is

uneven, so I bump up and down, finding it hard to focus on the obstacle course ahead. I start careering down the slope. As the car really starts to gather speed, the wind blows through the smashed windscreen like a gale. It's painful to keep my eyes open. Squinting, I wrench around the steering-wheel to avoid a huge boulder, then I veer round the other way, narrowly missing a tree. I'm terrified.

I glance up at the mirror, but the others have disappeared from view. The car is really picking up speed now and I can't see where the drop is. I'll have to get ready to jump. I push on the car door so that it's open, ready, but the door is stuck. I'd forgotten how squashed it got in the crash and it's all lop-sided. There's another boulder looming up, so I can't even look at the door and see what's wrong. I swerve to the right and miss the boulder.

I can see where the ground comes to a halt a short distance in front of me. I have to get out. I take both hands from the steering-wheel and push the door. It still won't give. I need to put more weight behind it. I try again. The door swings open. There's an onrush of wind from the side of me. I put one hand back on the steering-wheel to manoeuvre the car round another tree and then alter my feet so that I'm ready to jump. The car door is in the way so I have to leap out backwards. I know that's dangerous and I'm likely to injure myself, but there's no alternative. I take a deep breath and shove myself as hard as I can. I mustn't let the car drag me along with it to the drop. I leap as far away as possible. As I fly through the air, I let out a noise, not a scream, but an animal-like howl of fear. The next thing I know is that I've landed. The car has gone. I raise myself to run and watch it go crashing over the edge, but my legs give way beneath me. I collapse back down on the grass.

★

I can't allow myself the luxury of lying still for very long; I have to get up. My body feels like shredded sponge. I stagger tentatively to my feet, expecting at any second to shatter into a thousand fragments like a smattered animal on a TV cartoon. I think I'm still intact. I force my legs to totter gingerly down towards the drop, following the tracks the car has made in the grass. I look over the edge. The car is crumpled at the bottom like a battered Matchbox toy. I've done it. The car is dead. I turn and struggle back up the slope.

The others are waiting at the top. I'm expecting Julie to run down the hill and meet me, to throw her arms around me, thankful I'm still alive, but she doesn't. She's busy talking to Trevor and Mike. She doesn't even turn her head to look at me until I'm level with them.

'You left it a bit late, didn't you?' she says. She doesn't marvel at my bravery, she just sounds critical as if I've done something stupid.

'The car door wouldn't open.' When I think about how near I came to death, I want to cry.

I don't want them to see how upset I am. 'I'll have to be setting off,' I mumble and begin trudging along by the side of the road. The others follow a short way behind, still conferring together as though I don't exist.

I prefer to walk by myself. I feel shocked and stunned. I can't hear what they're discussing but, from the sound of their voices, it's nothing important. I've narrowly escaped from death and I just can't bring myself to chatter about trivia. I feel alone again and isolated. I need to shamble home in silence.

Ten minutes later, I reach the junction near the chip shop. I turn and wait a few moments for the others. 'We'll have to get off and look at the van,' says Trevor. 'We'd better make sure it's all right.'

'We'll phone up about a new tyre,' Mike adds.

I pause. I'm expecting them to apologize about the car. The least they could do is ask if I've recovered yet from the fall. There's an uncomfortable silence. I don't think they're even going to say that they hope my dad's not had a heart attack.

'I'll get off home, then,' I mutter. I still pause, hoping for some sort of consolation. I glance at Julie, but she's just gazing down at her boots.

'Right then.' I turn my head round quickly. I feel lost and alienated from them. I don't want them to notice that my eyes are filled with tears. 'I'll see you around,' I say, as casually as I can manage.

I turn and walk back home to meet my father.

20

When I walk inside the kitchen, there's no smell of dinner cooking. That's only happened once before, the day my grandad died. Apart from Saturdays when we have salad and when we've been away on holiday, my mother's cooked a meal for us every day of my life.

The kitchen is cold. The missing meal permeates the atmosphere of the house like a laid-out corpse. We're mourning the death of my father's car.

I don't know if they'll notice that I'm only wearing my T-shirt. I carry my jacket, as always, folded over my arm with the studs on the inside. I walk inside the living-room, trying to look bright and normal. 'Hello there,' I say. I give a bright breezy smile. 'Where's the car?'

There's silence. Just a stunned, painful, awful silence. My father stares down at the carpet and shakes his head. My mother looks up at me for a moment, then her lip trembles and she buries her head in her hands.

'What's the matter?' I ask.

I walk across and place my hand on my mother's shoulder. I can't actually bring myself to cuddle her, but I don't want to seem callous. I pause a few moments, touching her, waiting for them to find the strength to break the news I already know.

I'm expecting my father to speak, but he doesn't. He just stares down at the roses on the carpet. It's my mother who forces herself to tell me. She looks up, sniffing, and wipes her eyes with a hankie. 'Somebody's taken Dad's car,' she says. 'They came and took it whilst I was polishing the best silver and I didn't hear a thing. I didn't notice it was missing until I went to peg out the washing.'

I can't really think what to say without it sounding false and stupid. I struggle to think how I'd react if I didn't know about the car already. 'That's dreadful!' I pause for a moment. 'Have you contacted the police?' I ask.

'Dad phoned them up when he got home.'

'You should have told them straightaway.'

'Well . . .' My mother shakes her head. 'I'm no good at talking to policemen. Your father's better at things like that. And I thought he might have come and taken it for work . . .'

'Now, you know I wouldn't do that without so much as saying hello . . .' My father looks directly at me for the first time. I force myself to meet his eyes. 'What worries me so much, Christopher,' he confides, 'is that your mother was in by herself and somebody must have walked in . . . walked straight into the house and just taken the keys from the hall.'

'And I never heard a thing,' my mother sobs into her hankie.

'How anybody could do a thing like that I just don't know . . .' My father is overcome with emotion. He doesn't cry. He just puts his head down in his hands and gives up.

I'd feel so much better, if he were angry. If he were ranting and raving the way he did when the garden gnomes went astray, I could secretly mock him. I just feel sorry for him now.

'I don't know how I can leave your mother in the house by herself any more . . .'

I can't think what to say to that. 'Would you like a cup of tea?' I offer.

'That'd be lovely, Christopher.'

As I turn to walk into the kitchen, my jacket catches on the side of a chair and something falls out of the pocket. There's a small clatter. I look down and see the car keys lying on the carpet.

'Have you dropped something?'

My mother can't see them from where she's sitting. They're just out of sight around the corner of the chair.

'I've dropped some loose change out of my pocket,' I say, grinning foolishly. I'd forgotten that I still had the keys. They stare at me accusingly.

'It didn't sound like change. Do you want me to help you?'

'No, it's all right, thanks.' I pick up the keys and place them back inside my pocket. 'I've got it all now.'

I walk into the kitchen and put the kettle on. Whilst it's boiling, I go upstairs to fetch a sweater out of my drawer. I have an ominous feeling about the sweater as I put it on, as though there's something I should have worked out in my mind, but I can't think what it is. The telephone rings. I hurry downstairs to answer it.

'Hello.'

'Hello. Can I speak to Chris, please?'

'Speaking.'

'Hi. It's Sarah.'

'Oh.' I feel an onrush of affection for Sarah. I hug the receiver. 'Hi.'

'Are you all right?'

I pause. I'm not all right. I still feel shocked and weak and frightened, and I desperately need someone to talk to. 'Yes, I'm fine.' Another pause. 'Why?'

'Your voice sounded a bit strained, you know . . . as if you were upset.'

It's comforting to feel that Sarah cares about me, even if I can't tell her what it is that's wrong. 'No, I'm O.K.,' I tell her. 'How are you?'

'I'm fine. I've just finished typing out the stuff for the leaflet . . .'

'Oh, good.'

'You said you might be able to come round and collect it.'

'Yes, I will do.'

'If that's no trouble. I mean, I don't want to put you out . . .'

'No, it's no trouble.' Pause. 'It'll be nice to see you again.'

Sarah gives a tiny laugh as though she's embarrassed. 'Well, I enjoyed talking to you the other night.'

'Yes, I enjoyed it, too.'

'I hope I didn't bore you . . .'

'No,' I tell her. 'It's good to talk to somebody with a

different point of view. I've thought a lot about what you were saying . . .'

'Hey, did you hear the report on the news about the riot?'

'Er . . .' I don't know what to say.

'This riot in Bedgar. You weren't there, were you?'

Pause.

'Yes, I was there.'

'Oh.' Sarah sounds disappointed. 'Well, you'll have to tell me about it . . .'

'When are you free?'

'Tonight? Tomorrow?'

I'd like to see Sarah tonight, but I don't think I ought to go out and leave my mum and dad. It would look less suspicious if I stayed at home and helped them sort things out about the car. 'Tomorrow would be fine,' I tell her.

'I'll see you tomorrow evening, then. About half seven?'

'O.K. I'll look forward to seeing you.'

'O.K. Bye.'

'Bye, Sarah.'

The kettle's steaming away as I go into the kitchen to make the tea. I take out the best cups and arrange them neatly on a tray with the sugar bowl and biscuit tin. I pour milk into a jug instead of taking it in in the bottle and carry the tray through into the living-room.

'Well, now Christopher's home, I'll be able to walk down to the police station,' my father says. 'I told them I'd come along and give them all the particulars.'

I pour out the tea into the Spring Snot cups.

'I'll call round at the doctor's as well,' he tells my mum. 'I'll ask him for some of those tablets that you had when Grandad died.'

I look at my watch. 'The surgery closed half an hour ago,' I tell him.

'Oh, he won't mind. It's an emergency, isn't it?'

I dread to think what the doctor will say about my father banging on the door asking for Valium for my mum just because his car's been nicked. I think I ought to put him off. 'It's only a car,' I tell him.

My father looks at me in amazement. 'What do you mean?'

I wish straightaway that I'd not said it. 'Well, it's just a car . . . It's not as if . . . well, when you were talking about Grandad . . . it's not as if somebody's died.' I hesitate. I don't know whether it's right to try and make him look on the bright side of things or not. 'You can always buy another car . . .' I offer.

My father frowns at me. I pass him his cup of tea and a biscuit and give him a weak smile.

He still looks daggers at me. 'You don't understand, Christopher,' he says, taking the teacup from me. 'It's not the car I'm worried about. As you say, we can always buy another car. What we can't replace is your mother's peace of mind.'

I pass my mother her cup of tea.

'Knowing that someone has entered the house and taken the keys whilst your mother was on her own—anything could have happened. She could have been viciously attacked or . . .' He sits and shakes his head, then sips his tea.

It makes me sorry that what I've done has made him think he's not looking after my mother properly. I never realized how much they cared about each other.

'I don't know how I can go to work and leave her on her own . . .'

My mother doesn't say anything. The car keys are still

in my jacket pocket and I've left that in the kitchen. I must remember to hide them somewhere or throw them away.

'You'll be staying in tonight, won't you?' Dad asks. 'I don't want to leave your mother on her own whilst I go down and see the police.'

'That's all right. I'll be staying in.'

'Good.'

My father finishes his tea, then stands up and goes to collect his coat. When he comes back, he gently places his arm on my mother's shoulder. 'Try not to worry,' he tells her. 'You'll be all right with Christopher here.'

My mother looks up at him. 'Will you take the torch?' she says. 'It'll be dark when you come back. You don't know who there'll be walking about.'

My father leaves the house. When he's gone, I remember what it was that worried me about the sweater. I left my other sweater on the front seat of the car. It's not the kind of jumper you buy in a shop—it's one my mother knitted for me. If my father ever finds the car, he'll see my jumper lying on the front seat and he'll know that I was driving it.

21

Sarah invites me into the house and takes me through into the kitchen for some coffee. She makes it with a contraption of filter papers and a jug. We have instant coffee at our house, but Sarah's tastes much better.

We carry our mugs through into the room we were in before. I sit on the carpet, feeling more at ease than I did last time. I'm pleased when Sarah sits on the floor just opposite, leaning backwards against the arm of a chair. She puts down her coffee for a moment and shows me the leaflet.

I read it through. It's beautifully typed and the arguments are put over simply but very clearly. Sarah seems very competent. I can imagine her typing out things like this for her dad. 'It's very good,' I tell her. 'You've done a fantastic job.'

'You think it's O.K.?'

I'm pleased that she wants my opinion, that what I think is important to her. 'Yes,' I tell her. 'I'll take it to the printer's tomorrow.'

There's a pause for a while as we sit and drink our coffee. I know that Sarah's going to ask me about the riot and I haven't made my mind up what to tell her. I'd like to be able to unload my mind and tell her everything about the car and the policeman and the way I felt so sick about it all, but I still don't know Sarah well enough. I don't know how she'd react.

'We had reporters from the radio round here yesterday,' she tells me. 'They came to ask Dad what he thought about the riot.'

'Yes. I heard it.'

Sarah pauses and drinks some more of her coffee. 'What did you think?'

'About the interview?'

She nods.

I take a deep breath. I have to come down on one side or the other. 'I think he was right,' I tell her. 'I agreed with everything he said.'

Sarah looks surprised. 'But I thought you said that you were there? You took part in it, didn't you?'

I drink some more coffee whilst I gather my thoughts. It's not easy to explain why I disagreed with the riot without telling her the reasons why. 'I *was* there,' I say, 'but just sort of . . . standing around on the sidelines.'

'Did you throw anything?'

'Not to hurt anybody.' I pause. 'I just threw a garden gnome.'

Sarah scoffs. 'A garden gnome! You just happened to have one handy, I suppose . . .'

I think how to change the subject. Whilst I'm wondering what to say, I notice a copy of Dylan Thomas lying on the table with a project folder next to it and a half-finished essay. 'You're not doing Dylan Thomas as well, are you?' I ask.

Sarah smiles. 'That's right. I'm just ploughing through this week's essay. Are you on the same course?'

'It looks like it.'

I move over closer to Sarah and pick up her book. I start leafing through it, mentioning the poems that I've been writing about and pointing out the parts I like. It's surprising to find that the two of us like the same poems. Both of us seem so very different: we come from completely different homes and backgrounds and yet, when it comes to poetry, there we are—reading the same stuff and writing the same kind of comments about it. We talk for quite a time about different poems—it's easier than talking about the peace movement and D.A.M.N. We have some more coffee and I start to feel much more relaxed. I realize that Sarah and I are getting on quite well.

It takes a bit of courage for me to pick up the book and read out loud to Sarah extracts from poems that I like, but which I've never read aloud before. Sarah sits on the carpet at my feet and listens attentively, nodding her head slowly in appreciation. 'That's lovely,' she tells me when I've finished the first poem, and I feel encouraged to read on.

I decide to read her my favourite poem; it's something I want to share with her. I find it in the book and start to read out loud:

> 'Do not go gentle into that good night,
> Old age should burn and rave at close of day;
> Rage, rage against the dying of the light . . .'

I read on and Sarah listens contentedly. When I've finished there's a pause. I look at my watch. I don't want to overstay my welcome. 'I ought to be getting home,' I tell her.

There's silence for a few moments. I'd like to be able to see Sarah again, but I'm not sure how to suggest it. I suddenly start to feel awkward. I was going to suggest that we went round giving out leaflets together, but I don't think they'll be ready from the printer's for another week.

'Will you be at the meeting next week?' she asks me.

I'd forgotten about that. 'Yes, are you going?'

Sarah purses her lips. 'Yes . . .' she answers thoughtfully.

I wait for her to carry on.

'I'm putting forward a vote of no-confidence in the officers.'

There's a moment's silence.

'What do you mean?'

'Quite a few of us were talking about it . . .' Sarah takes a sip of her coffee. She seems uncertain whether she ought to be telling me this or not. 'My dad, Mr and Mrs Wheatley . . .'

'Helen Wheatley's parents?'

'That's right. Dad's on the board of managers with Mr Wheatley at the school.'

'Oh, I didn't know that.'

'Anyway, they've been getting quite fed up with the

way Ralph's chairing the meetings. Stewart might be coming out of hospital soon, so that might get Ralph out of the way. They suggested putting my name forward as the new Secretary instead of Julie.'

'I see.'

Sarah would make a good Secretary. She's obviously capable and efficient and she'd probably be popular with most of the others in the group, but I dread to think what D.A.M.N. would have to say about it.

Sarah smiles at me hesitantly. 'I wanted to be open about it,' she says. 'I don't like to think of machinations taking place behind the scenes . . .'

I nod my head slowly. 'Would you be able to cope with the work?' I ask her. 'I mean, you'll have your homework to do and everything.'

'I've thought about it,' says Sarah. 'I'm used to hard work. I help Dad with the elections. I don't have much . . . social life,' she adds quietly. 'Not compared with most girls my age.'

There's silence for a few seconds. 'Why not?' I ask.

Sarah takes a deep breath. 'I just don't get invited out to places. I think it's mainly that . . . well, I used to be at a private boarding-school, but I didn't like it, and I asked Dad if I could go to the local comprehensive instead.'

'Why were you at a boarding-school?' I ask her.

'I went to the local primary school until I was eleven. Then Mum and Dad split up. Dad thought he wouldn't be able to look after me properly—when he's away at conferences and meetings. He thought it would be easier if I just stayed here in the holidays.'

'I see.' I'd wondered why I hadn't seen anything of Sarah's mum, but I hadn't liked to ask her about it. 'Don't you like it any better at the comprehensive, then?'

'The school's a lot better,' she explains. 'It's just that I feel as though people think I'm a bit odd. Living in a big house and being the daughter of an M.P.—it sort of . . . puts people off me, if you know what I mean. I suppose they think I must be snobbish or posh or something.'

I smile at her. I want to say something reassuring. 'It's what you're like as a person that counts,' I tell her. 'I'd have thought you were easy to get on with.'

I don't know whether Sarah's saying all this just to unload what's on her mind, or whether—and I can hardly bring myself to think of this as a possibility—whether, in fact, she's giving me a cue to ask her out. 'I feel a bit like that with the kids I go to school with,' I tell her. 'I don't mean that they think I'm snobbish, but . . . well, I feel sort of . . . apart from them. I can't share things with them. I mean, I can't talk about politics with them or poetry—except in lessons, of course, but that's different.'

Sarah smiles and nods. I feel very warm towards her. I'd like to be able to touch her or hug her, but I can't bring myself to do it.

It's time for me to go. I stand up. The silence is there between us again. I try to think of something else to say to bring us nearer to establishing some more definite relationship, but the words aren't there. The air is heavy with unspoken thoughts.

I pick up Sarah's typescript. 'I'll take this to the printer's tomorrow,' I say.

'O.K.'

I walk out of the room towards the front door, hoping that by the time I reach it all the other things I want to say will have formed themselves into words. But no. We stand together on the front step. Unspoken thoughts flutter in the space between us like a flock of invisible swifts, afraid of settling on to anything more solid than the darkness.

I reach across and touch Sarah on the arm. Her body

feels soft and gentle. I breathe in the scent of her perfume. I want to remember it after I've gone. She takes my hand in hers and we stand there for a second or two, each of us looking at the ground between us. I squeeze her fingers slightly, but her hand is brittle and slender like the body of a baby bird. I feel afraid of hurting her. I let go of her hand. 'Good-night.'

'Good-night.'

I go gently down the driveway into the night.

22

I wake up from dreaming that I've been making love to Sarah. The dream is such a deeply sensual experience that I struggle hopelessly to rescue it, driving at the scanner in my brain to seek out and solidify the residue of pictures, the shadows of sensations that leave my body throbbing still with pleasure. The dream has gone. I feel as though I came so near to touching something completely above and beyond myself, a pinnacle of experience, that I can hardly bear to admit to myself that I'm aching for the memory of an experience that doesn't, in reality, exist.

I get out of bed and dress myself. I try to shake the dream away from me. I try to tell myself that it was meaningless, a flood of thoughts and emotions associated with Sarah for no other reason than that I'd been with her most of the evening. I don't manage to convince myself. Emotions that I can't explain are pulsing through my brain as I struggle for the umpteenth time to fasten up the buttons on my shirt. I have a scary feeling that I might be falling in love with Sarah.

I sit down at the breakfast table, stirring my tea and gazing in bewilderment at little chunks of marmalade, circling round my cup where the tea leaves ought to be.

'Christopher,' my father tells me, 'you've just stirred a spoonful of marmalade into your tea.'

'Oh.' That explains it.

'And your shirt's on inside out,' my mother informs me.

I study the front of my shirt and, with a splutter of insight, see why it's taken me so long to fasten up the buttons. I drink some tea. It doesn't taste too bad with marmalade in.

My father's gazing at me querulously as if I'm a pubescent gnome he's found wandering around the rockery. 'Were you out with all those radicals again last night?' he asks me.

I can't decide whether an evening at the Barnforth's counts as being *out with all those radicals again* or not. 'How do you mean?' I ask him.

'I was reading in the paper about the effects of all this drug abuse. Teenagers getting distracted from their school work with smoking glue and sniffing ESP . . .'

Sniffing ESP?

'. . . apparently they do all sorts of stupid things,' he explains, glaring suspiciously at the chunks of marmalade floating round my tea cup. 'They don't even know what day of the week it is. It said how parents have to be on the look-out for any signs of abnormal behaviour.'

I look across at my mother eating her scrambled egg. That means it must be Friday. Other people tell the day of the week by their calendar or their watch; we tell what day it is by the shape of our eggs in the morning. 'It all depends on what you mean by normal,' I tell him.

My mother and father look at each other in confusion. Normal, to them, is simply what they do and how they live their lives. Anything else is abnormal and it's wrong.

I decide to change the subject. 'Is there any news yet from the police?' I ask. I don't really want to keep talking about the car, but I know it'll look suspicious if I never even mention it.

My father just shakes his head. He doesn't say anything.

I try to think of something optimistic to say about the car, but my brain is distracted by the picture of it, wrecked and battered in the dried-up stream. There's nothing I can think of to console him. I stand up from the table. 'I'll go and change my shirt,' I tell them.

I set off for school still feeling disoriented, my mind refusing to disengage itself from the fact that it thinks I've spent the night making love to Sarah. I find it hard to concentrate. I manage registration and Assembly, but then I lose track of what I'm supposed to be doing and wander into the changing-rooms to get ready for cross country.

It dawns on me eventually that the kids I'm with are a whole lot smaller than I am and I realize that my class must be somewhere else. I saunter down to the cookery rooms in my shorts and football socks and see the other kids from my class, stirring minced meat and cooking potatoes.

Helen Wheatley stops mashing her potatoes and stares so long at my naked thighs that smoke starts twirling from her saucepan. 'What on earth are you doing?' she asks me.

'I thought it was Games.'

'In the cookery room?' She gapes at me in amazement.

I just shrug my shoulders at her.

Helen looks at me as if I've just escaped from a top security mental home. 'It's cottage pie this week,' she explains reprovingly.

Oh no. Don't say I've missed the first opportunity in my life to learn how to cook my very own cottage pie. I can't face it.

I make a superhuman effort to control my thoughts better in the afternoon. In English I try to write an essay about Dylan Thomas and 'Fern Hill' but, when I try to study the text of the poem, looking up at me out of the book are scenes of Sarah and myself running along Fern Hill, holding hands and laughing.

For the hundredth time, I press the courser in my brain and send it scanning backwards and forwards across the mental screen, deleting pictures of a non-existent Sarah and hallucinatory Chris walking through fictitious fern-filled forests. And still they reappear, superimposed across the printed page, wandering in and out of purple sunsets like spectres passing backwards and forwards through locked and bolted doors. I can't get rid of them. And it's all so ludicrous because I've never even liked walking in the countryside and I've never got hyped up about sunsets and all that stuff. My only consolation is that it's keeping my mind distracted from worrying about the car.

At home that evening I get a phone call from Mike. 'The cops are keeping Ralph locked up,' he tells me.

I was assuming Ralph would be back at home by now. 'Won't they let him out on bail?' I ask. 'I mean, he's not been in trouble before or anything, has he?'

Mike laughs out loud. 'Not been in trouble!' he scoffs. 'They've got his face up on a bloody Wanted poster.'

I feel staggered at that. I wouldn't have been surprised to find that Mike or Trevor had been in trouble, but not Ralph. They usually only put people's faces on a poster if they're wanted for murder or terrorism or something.

They must have got him mixed up with somebody else.

'Anyway,' says Mike, 'he won't be back for the meeting next week so I'm going to chair it.'

'Good idea.'

'I'm just worried that we'll get some hassle about the riot. I thought we could spin out all the other items to make sure there isn't time left for a debate.'

'I see.'

'I thought you could give a report about that jumble sale—do you think you could stretch it out for about twenty minutes . . . ?'

Twenty minutes! I don't know what I can say about the jumble sale that'll last for more than two minutes, let alone twenty. 'I can have a try.'

'What do you think, Chris? Do you think there'll be any come-back about the stuff at Bedgar?'

I pause. 'I think there'll be some problems from the Animal Lovers against the Bomb group—you know, old Miss Meadows and her mates . . .'

'Yeah, but we should be able to shut them up. I was wondering whether Barnforth might be turning up. Have you heard anything, Chris? I know Ralph asked you to go round and see Sarah . . .'

I hesitate. 'Yes. They had a meeting the other night.'

'Who did?'

'Sarah and her dad, a bloke called Wheatley and some others.'

'Bloody typical. If they've got things to say, then why can't they say them at proper meetings instead of having secret bloody discussions . . .'

I feel like pointing out to him that we're having a secret discussion now, but I decide against it. 'Sarah said they were thinking of putting forward a no-confidence vote in

Ralph and Julie; well in Julie really, because they said Stewart might be out of hospital before too long . . .'

'You what? Stewart coming out of hospital?'

'That's right.'

Mike sounds amazed. 'That car crash should've bloody killed him.'

I don't know if I should have mentioned to Mike what Sarah told me, but she did say that she didn't want people to think that she was being secretive.

'You making out with Sarah, then?' Mike asks me. His voice is cold and suspicious.

I'm not sure what he's getting at. I try to make sure I sound casual, as if I couldn't care less about Sarah. 'I'm doing O.K.,' I answer.

There's another pause. I feel as though I've said the wrong thing to Mike, but I'm not sure why.

Mike takes a breath as if he's about to say something else, but then seems to change his mind. He waits for a second or two.

'I'll put the report about the jumble sale as the first item on the agenda,' he tells me. 'I'll leave it up to you how long you spin it out.'

I had thought about telling them all that I didn't want to be in involved with D.A.M.N. any more, but it doesn't seem the right time at the moment. 'O.K.'

'I'll see you at the meeting then, Chris . . .'

'O.K.'

'Cheers.'

'Cheers, Mike.'

I replace the receiver. Mike never even asked about the car. I have an uncomfortable feeling that he couldn't care less whether I get into trouble for it or not.

23

The first person that I notice when I walk into the upstairs room at The Black Bull on Monday is Sarah. As soon as I see her, something inside me melts. I don't know what it is, but it must be something important because straightaway I feel a whole lot weaker than when I walked up the stairs. Sarah looks up at me and smiles, then she turns away as if she's embarrassed. I feel a tiny glimmer of hope that maybe she feels the same as I do.

Sitting next to Sarah are Helen Wheatley and Lee Furgusson. Helen seems to think that my smile is intended for her. She grins at me from ear to ear and bounces up and down in her seat like a wallaby on its birthday.

I have to walk past them anyway and sit next to Mike at the front of the room to give my report about the jumble sale. Mike tells everyone that Ralph is otherwise engaged and so has asked him to chair the meeting. There are no actual complaints, although a few people give him dirty looks. Mike then explains that, although we've had one meeting since the jumble sale, it's taken me all this time to write my report about it, so that's going to be the first item on tonight's agenda.

I've written four pages about the jumble sale. First of all, I list all the items of expenditure. I mention the cost of hiring the hall at so much an hour, the tip we gave the caretaker, the exact number of tea bags used, the milk and everything else I can think of, including the price of half a stick of chalk for writing on the blackboard outside the Revival Hall. I don't manage to spin out the report for twenty minutes, but I keep it going for so long that some of the more elderly campaigners look as if they've fallen asleep.

'Thank you very much,' Mike says, when I've finished. 'I'm sure we all want to congratulate Chris on writing such a thorough and comprehensive report.' He looks around at the circle of bored and apathetic faces. They stare back at him, as bemused as a coven of dead goldfish.

'Right then,' says Mike, 'we'll move on to talk about the Ryecroft demonstration.'

Mike's report is about six times longer than mine. It's been generally accepted that the march we held in Ryecroft and the rally in the Civic Hall were both a great success. Mike plays on this, trying to make out that the whole campaign has really gained momentum since Ralph took over as Chairman. Actually, I think Stewart organized most of the demonstration before he went into hospital, but nobody mentions that.

The first criticism about the demo comes from Mrs Hardacre. 'I was most unhappy about the leaflets produced for the demonstration,' she says. 'What we write on leaflets ought to reflect the views of the peace group. There are quite a few of us—most of us, in fact—who disagree strongly with the Direct Action against the Missiles Now group and we want our views made clear. I think we ought to talk about all this trouble last Wednesday and those policemen who were injured. I'd like us to put out a statement saying we want to disassociate ourselves from hooliganism like that.'

There are shouts of, 'Well said!' and 'Hear, hear!' The meeting starts to liven up.

'Well, I'll put that down under Any Other Business,' Mike says, 'but there are a couple more items on the agenda that have to be covered first.'

Miss Meadows stands up. 'As a representative of Animal Lovers against the Bomb,' she croaks, 'I think we should have a full enquiry into . . .'

'Look,' Mike interrupts her, 'I've put that down under Any Other Business. Can we please leave it until then and get the other items dealt with first?'

There are mutterings of discontent from all around the room.

Mike starts looking agitated. 'Look, if I can just mention what you were saying about the leaflets,' he explains. 'Ralph asked Sarah Barnforth to produce the next one for us, working . . .' he turns round and points at me . . . 'working in co-operation with Chris, here. I hope you think that's all right.'

'I hope it's not as long as that report about the jumble sale,' says Harry, 'or people will be falling asleep before they're halfway through it.'

Mike scowls at Harry in disgust. 'Is the leaflet nearly ready?' he asks me.

'Yes.' I glance across at Sarah and smile at her. 'Sarah's done most of it. It's very good.'

'There you are,' says Mike, 'we do take account of any . . . constructive criticisms that people want to make.'

Miss Meadows hasn't sat down yet. 'I heard that a tortoise was thrown at a policeman,' she grumbles. She hasn't completed her speech; she's just been gathering her thoughts. 'Now, I don't actually agree with tortoises being brought over here out of their natural habitat. Many of them find it hard to survive an English winter, but that's no excuse for . . .'

'Miss Meadows!' Mike shouts across at her. 'We've noted that for discussion later on. Will you please sit down and let us get on?'

Someone has a word with Miss Meadows and she sits

down, looking very upset and still muttering away to herself.

'Now,' says Mike, 'can we talk about the arrangements for the next public meeting?'

He goes on to explain that one of the local churches has offered us free use of their hall for the next big meeting and several speakers have been invited, including Bevan Barnforth. Mike then stalls for time again, going through all the arrangements about who's going to make the tea and whether we ought to serve Co-op shortcakes with the tea or charge people extra and give them chocolate digestives.

'Well,' says Julie, 'there are lots of people out of work who might find it offensive if the only biscuits on sale are outside their price range.'

'There are plenty of old-age pensioners on low incomes as well,' adds Mike.

'And school kids,' I butt in.

'On the other hand,' says Mike, 'we don't want to look as if we're doing everything on the cheap.' He looks round the circle of disgusted faces. 'Has anyone any other suggestions?'

Helen Wheatley raises her hand. I think she's the only one who's still paying any attention.

'Yes?'

'I think we ought to compromise by having Custard Creams,' she giggles, then curls up in embarrassment at having made such a major speech in public.

'Good idea,' says Mike. 'Right, we'll take a vote on it, then. Co-op shortcakes, chocolate digestives or Custard Creams . . . ?'

Just a handful of people put up their hands to vote. The rest that are still awake look at each other and raise their eyebrows in disgust.

'That's four votes for Co-op shortcakes, three for chocolate digestives, two for Custard Creams and thirty-four abstentions.'

'Just a minute,' Julie complains. 'I only counted thirty-eight people here. We can't have anomalies like that in the minutes. We'll have to have a recount.'

Mike pretends he hasn't heard the groans that are resounding quite openly now around the room. 'Right, will you put up your hands again, please. Those in favour of Co-op shortcakes . . . ?'

By the time the rest of the agenda has been covered, there are only five or six minutes left. 'Now,' says Mike, 'any other urgent business?'

Sarah stands up to speak. In her hand she's holding a sheet of typewritten notes. Although her voice is soft, she speaks clearly enough to be heard around the room. 'Yes, I would like to put forward a vote of no-confidence in the officers of the meeting,' she says.

Mike's jaw sets hard. 'I don't think we've time for that,' he says curtly. 'We've only . . .'

The rest of his sentence is drowned as people shout out in derision. Then there are cries of, 'Listen to Sarah!' and 'Let her speak!'

Sarah waits for the noise to die down, but she doesn't wait for Mike's permission to continue. She looks up from her notes. 'This meeting has been an absolute shambles,' she exclaims in exasperation. 'The campaign to get rid of the missiles is an urgent one, not a long-term project. We don't have time to sit around discussing the price of tea bags, sticks of chalk . . .' she looks at me pointedly . . . 'or debating about the cost of biscuits . . .'

'Hear! Hear!' shouts Mrs Hardacre. A few people applaud. Mike doesn't have any option but to sit back and let Sarah carry on.

Sarah pauses for a moment, turning slightly so that she can speak to everyone in the room. 'What's most important,' she says seriously, 'is that when officers of our campaign take part in the kind of activities that get us overwhelming bad publicity, they undo everything that we've been working for. All the work we've done over the past few years in leafleting and holding peaceful demonstrations is completely wasted, if it results in people associating us with a riot like the one in Bedgar last week.'

More applause. It's obvious that, even though Sarah's only young, people take her seriously and she's very popular. I can understand them wanting to put her forward as the new Secretary.

Mike lights a cigarette and begins to break up the matchstick into pieces. 'We can't discuss this any further,' he says. 'We have to be out of this room in . . .'

There's an uproar from the meeting. They won't let him get away with that. Mike looks round helplessly at Trevor, Julie and myself, but none of us can think of anything to say.

Sarah stays on her feet, waiting for some acknowledgement of what she's just said. Then Miss Meadows stands up. 'If I may speak on behalf of the Animal Lovers against the Bomb group,' she croaks, 'I think we should . . .'

'Oh, sit down, you stupid old bag,' shouts Mike.

There's immediate silence. Several people half-rise out of their seats as if they're about to rush forward and lynch Mike. He's said the worst thing he possibly could to put everybody against him.

Sarah takes immediate advantage of the silent hostility. She speaks calmly and resolutely. 'If the Chairperson refuses to act upon what I've said, then can I please ask for a vote? Will all those who support the vote of no-confidence in the officers please raise their hands . . .'

Almost everyone in the room puts up their hands. I bend down and start twiddling with the laces on my shoes. I don't want Sarah to think I'm not supporting her, but I don't see how I can when I'm sitting here next to Mike.

'This is out of order,' yells Mike.

Sarah glares at him. 'Why is it?'

'Because we don't have all the officers present, that's why. You can't put forward a vote of no-confidence in the official Chairman unless he's here to answer it. It'll have to be deferred until the next meeting.'

The meeting erupts again into groans and expressions of disgust, but I think Mike's won his case. Harry stands up. 'Can I suggest then,' he says, 'that we call a special emergency meeting for this time next week for the Chairman to answer any criticisms and for us to discuss the relationship between the Ryecroft peace group and members of D.A.M.N.? I'd like to suggest, in fact, that anyone who joins D.A.M.N. be immediately excluded from the peace group.'

'Yeah,' says Julie sarcastically. 'Let's have a full-scale witch-hunt. I'll recommend that all members of Animal Lovers against the Bomb be excluded as well. They're the biggest pain in the arse.'

Trevor grins at Julie and puts his arm on her shoulder. There's a special comradeship about being in a group like D.A.M.N. when you're working together against everyone else, but I don't feel that it's a friendship I can share with them any more. I think I'll have to talk to Sarah straight after the meeting and make sure she doesn't think that I'm against her as well.

'Look,' answers Mike, 'calling a special meeting means that we have to send a mailing to all the members. That's a very big job for the Secretary and a lot of extra postage. Stamps don't grow on trees, you know.'

'Well, I'd like to second what Harry's just said,' adds Mrs Hardacre. 'Can we have a vote on whether to hold an emergency meeting or not . . . ?'

Mike sighs and stubs out his cigarette on the table. 'O.K.,' he says resignedly. 'All those in favour of an emergency meeting . . .'

Nearly everyone raises their hand. I place my elbow on the table and raise my finger slightly, so it's not clear whether I'm voting or not.

'I suppose that's carried,' grumbles Mike. 'I'll inform the Chairman and we'll send out a mailing that the next meeting will be at the same time and place next week. All right?'

People nod grudgingly as they stand to leave the room.

Helen Wheatley rushes across to me as soon as the meeting's over. 'Hello, Chris,' she simpers. 'I thought I might see you here.'

'Hi.' I glance across at Sarah. She seems to be fully occupied with consoling Miss Meadows, who's dabbing at her eyes with a tissue. 'Can I buy you a drink?' I ask Helen. I think that's the best way of ensuring that Sarah joins me afterwards downstairs.

'Ooh! That would be nice.'

I lead Helen down into the bar and buy her a glass of shandy. I buy myself some beer. I'm getting used to drinking it now. As soon as Sarah comes downstairs, Helen yodels and beckons her across.

I stand up. 'What'll you have to drink, Sarah?'

Sarah looks at me reproachfully as if she's about to refuse. Then she seems to change her mind. 'I'll have a glass of orange juice, please,' she says.

'Are you sure? I mean, is that all?'

'Yes, thanks. That'll be fine. Oh, and I'll have a packet of crisps.'

I walk across to the bar.

'Thanks,' says Sarah, when I return with her drink and the crisps. I wait for her to smile at me but she doesn't.

I sit down opposite her and take a sip of my beer. 'You spoke very well,' I tell her. I smile at her tentatively but still there's no response.

'So did you.' Sarah's voice is cynical. 'At great length as well. It almost seemed as if you engineered all that,' she says. 'As if you'd all got together to delay my vote of no-confidence. I mean, I wonder how people could have found out about it . . .'

I could get into an argument with Sarah by reminding her that she did say she wanted to be open about everything, but I decide against it. I think it's best to change the subject.

'The leaflets should be ready tomorrow,' I tell her. 'I wondered if you might come with me to give some out . . .'

She hesitates, sipping slowly at the fruit juice. 'O.K.,' she says at last.

'I'll give you a ring tomorrow evening, then.' I don't want to make arrangements with her now in case Helen decides to tag along and help us.

Sarah nods. 'This is the leaflet I was telling you about,' she says to Helen. 'The one that Chris and I were both working on.'

Helen looks envious. 'I'm no good at things like that,' she says. 'I wish I was.'

'That's not true,' Sarah tells her. 'You can do anything if you put your mind to it.'

I don't think that would apply to Helen, although I can

see how it would with Sarah. I don't suppose there's much she's tried and failed at.

Mike and Trevor walk into the bar with Julie and Lee Furgusson. Julie takes Lee over to a table in the corner; Mike and Trevor buy their drinks then walk across and join us. No one invites them to sit down, but they do.

Sarah and Mike stare hostilely at each other. Mike lights up a cigarette and blows the smoke directly into Sarah's face. She doesn't flinch.

I gaze at Sarah's fingers, long and slender, entwined around the stem of her glass and I remember how she held my hand the other night. I wish I could touch her. I stretch out my leg towards her beneath the table until it makes contact with a shoe. Sarah doesn't look at me. 'What happened to Ralph tonight, then?' she asks Mike.

Mike takes a swig of his beer. 'He got arrested last week.'

'At Bedgar?'

He nods.

Sarah raises her eyebrows in a look of disgust. 'What's he being charged with?' she asks.

Mike looks at her straight in the eyes as if he's answering a challenge. He speaks slowly and unashamedly. 'Assaulting a police officer . . . resisting arrest . . . causing a breach of the peace . . . obstructing a police officer in the execution of his duty . . .'

Sarah looks unmoved and unimpressed. 'And I suppose you think that's done the peace movement a lot of good?'

Mike blows smoke into her face again. 'It's done more good than you and your father'll ever do. Somebody's got to smash the system.'

Sarah's furious. I can tell by the way she's breathing heavily and the way her fingers tighten around her glass, but she doesn't want Mike to see that he's antagonized her.

She's trying not to lose her cool. 'You know quite well that violence won't do the campaign any good,' she tells Mike reproachfully. 'You're into that because you enjoy it—the campaign against the missiles is just an excuse for a punch-up, as far as you're concerned.'

'It's as good an excuse as any,' Mike answers.

Sarah sits and seethes. There's an uncomfortable silence. 'Aren't you sharing out your crisps?' Helen asks her brightly.

Sarah slides them across the table. 'You can have them,' she answers. 'I don't feel like eating any more.'

'Crisps, anybody?' Helen chirrups, handing them round the table. Trevor and I just shake our heads. Mike puts his whole hand into the crisp bag, brings it out full of crisps and rams them all into his mouth at once. He sits chewing them noisily with his mouth open.

'Well, you might have left me some,' Helen whines, tipping the crumbs from the empty bag on to the palm of her hand.

I know that Mike's being obnoxious on purpose just to antagonize Sarah. It's as if he's deliberately taunting her, trying to get some reaction. I struggle to think of other topics to change the conversation on to, but I don't know where to start.

Mike swills the remnants of his crisps down with a mouthful of beer, then wipes the froth from his mouth with the sleeve of his leather jacket. He looks up at Sarah again. 'You telling me we don't live in a violent world, then?' he asks her.

'Of course there's violence,' Sarah answers, 'but we have to oppose it, not condone it. It's up to us to show that it's possible to find peaceful solutions to conflict—that you don't need weapons to gain respect from people.'

'That's a load of crap,' says Mike.

Sarah sighs deeply and clenches her teeth.

'Pacifism's all right in theory,' Mike goes on, 'but it doesn't work in practice. Supposing somebody attacked you, and Trev and I were around, you'd expect us to help you out . . . ?'

Sarah looks up at him. 'It's not as simple as that . . .'

'Oh, come on.' Mike's not going to let her get away with that. 'Say you were walking home on your own tonight and some guy jumped out on you and tried to rape you. If we were within earshot, then you'd call on us for help. Right?'

Sarah shrugs. 'Probably, but that's not . . .'

'And if it took a bit of aggro to get this guy sorted out, then you're not going to start complaining . . .'

Sarah thinks about it for a moment. 'I can't say what I'd do. As I said before, it's not as simple as that . . .'

'Of course it's bloody simple!' Mike scoffs. 'You can talk about bloody pacifism till the cows come home, but when you're threatened with violence, then you have to use violence back. There's nothing more aggressive than a bloody government armed to the teeth with nuclear missiles and, if you need a bit of aggro to oppose it, then we're going to have to get some in. Right, Trev?'

'Right.'

I'm pleased Mike doesn't ask me what I think. I wouldn't know what to say.

Sarah sips pensively at her orange juice. She glances up at Mike and gives him a cynical smile. 'I'll tell you what it all boils down to,' she says scathingly. 'It's little boys playing soldiers. That's what war's about and that's what D.A.M.N.'s about.'

'Oh, fuck off.'

There's a deathly silence. I know Mike's trying to shock Sarah, but she isn't rising to the bait. She looks down at her glass for a moment and then raises it and finishes her drink. She appears to be completely composed, ice cool and relaxed. The only thing out of place is the tension in her little finger, its knuckle white with pressure against the stem of her glass. When she looks up again at Mike, her eyes are cold with contempt.

She reaches across and lightly touches the cuff of his black leather jacket. 'When blokes need to cower behind a macho image like D.A.M.N.,' she says derisively, 'they're usually trying to cover up their own inadequacies. The bully boys are the ones who are completely impotent.'

There's another ominous silence as hatred begins to erupt from Mike's face like pus from a perforated boil. He clenches his fists. Sarah ignores the tension. She continues with her voice as calm and self-assured as ever. 'The blokes who can make it,' she says, 'are those who never need to prove anything to anybody. Those who can't make it are the ones who never stop searching for ways of proving that they're men.'

Sarah looks straight at Mike to see whether her words have hit home. Mike's eyes are blazing. His jaw is set like an iron horseshoe. The silence is as cold and stark as tempered steel. All of us stare at him, waiting for the explosion.

Sarah doesn't give him chance. She stands up quickly. 'Come on, Helen,' she says. 'It's time we were going.'

Helen finishes her shandy. She forces her face into a grin, but none of us are relaxed enough to smile. We just stare at her as if she's stupid. As Helen stands and moves away from the table, I look down at her feet and realize that hers is the shoe I've been gently leaning my foot against. No wonder she's been so quiet.

'Well, good-night everybody,' Sarah says. Her voice is cold and formal.

I was intending to remind her about going out with me

to take the leaflets, but it doesn't seem appropriate.
'Good-night Sarah,' I say quietly.

None of the others speak to her.

Mike sits at the table like a granite gargoyle, staring at the door. Trevor reaches out his hand to touch him on the shoulder, then draws back. Lines of tension stand out as tightened creases in the leather of Mike's jacket. His body is as taut as a panther's, poised for the kill.

'Another drink, Mike?' Trevor asks him.

Mike says nothing.

'Chris?'

'I'll have another half, thanks, Trev,' I say. I try to make my voice sound normal. There's no way we can take back what Sarah's said to Mike; all we can do is try to return to normality as soon as possible.

'Mike?'

Mike doesn't turn his head but simply slides his empty glass across to Trevor. Trev picks up the glasses and strides across to the bar. I can't think what to say to Mike. I decide to take a trip to the Gents instead.

As I cross the room, I notice Julie chatting up Lee Furgusson. She's gazing up at him sexily and stroking her hand across his knee. I could hit her. I walk straight past them both and into the bog.

I don't feel jealous about Julie, but I'm still angry. I suppose Lee will be the next one wearing D.A.M.N. studs across his jacket.

As I walk back from the Gents, I see that Mike's still sitting on his own. I go and help Trevor to carry the drinks.

*

Mike is smoking a cigarette and chiselling lumps out of the plastic ashtray with his penknife. He looks up and takes the beer that Trevor passes him. 'Thanks,' he mutters.

I don't know whether he's back to normal yet or not.

'Do you think Ralph'll be here for this meeting next week?' Trevor asks, as he sits down.

Mike shrugs. 'Doubt it.'

'I don't think we can put them off with this debate,' says Trevor.

Mike swallows a few mouthfuls of beer. 'We can try.'

'No.' Trevor shakes his head. 'They've probably got somebody lined up to put forward as new Secretary or Chairman or maybe both. Although I can't think who they'd have . . .'

I thought I'd already told them about Sarah. 'They're putting Sarah forward as the new Secretary,' I explain.

Trev and Mike both stare at me incredulously. 'Who told you that?' asks Trevor.

'She did.'

'Bloody hell!' He shakes his head in disgust.

Mike is staring downwards, stabbing his knife into the ashtray. Trevor and I both look at him, waiting for his reaction. Mike is silent, then he looks up at us. 'We'll have to stop it happening,' he says.

'How do you mean?' asks Trevor.

Mike lights up another cigarette from the butt of his last one. He blows smoke across the table and stubs out the old cigarette. 'We'll stop her getting to the meeting,' he says.

Trevor looks across at me and I shrug my shoulders. I can't see what Mike's getting at.

Suddenly his face starts to brighten up. 'Look,' he says, 'I've got a plan.'

He gulps down some more of his beer. 'I've got a

fantastic idea,' he says. 'You know when I asked her what she'd do if some bloke tried to rape her . . . ?'

'Yeah . . .'

'We'll set it up.' Mike's face is animated. 'We rig up a situation where she's getting attacked . . . then, when she's really scared and yelling for somebody to help her out, that's when we turn up.'

Trevor and I frown at each other.

'We rescue Sarah,' Mike goes on, 'but only do it on condition that she agrees to us sorting this guy out. She has to sit back and watch us work him over.'

I can see the appeal of this for Mike. 'You mean, we'd be showing her how pacifism doesn't work?' I ask.

'That's right.'

I don't like the sound of it. 'Who'd attack Sarah, though,' I ask him, 'then stick around whilst we have a go at him?'

With a smug expression on his face, Mike puts down his glass of beer. 'That's easy,' he explains. 'The bloke'll be one of us.'

He must be mad. 'But Sarah would go to the police,' I object. 'None of us want to get done for attempted rape!'

'No,' says Mike, 'he can wear a disguise . . . like a horror mask and gloves and some kind of jacket, so she won't recognize who he is. It'll be dark anyway . . .'

I don't know whether Mike's serious or not.

'Who do you think's going to volunteer to get beaten up?' I ask. I glance at Trevor's huge frame, overhanging his flimsy stool like a performing elephant in a circus. 'An argument with Trev on his own would be bad enough without anyone else piling in.'

Mike grins. 'You don't understand what I'm getting at,' he says. 'None of us would get hurt. We'd have to do one of those stunt fights—like they have in all the Westerns.'

'I was in one of those in a school play.' As soon as I've said that, I wish I hadn't. I don't want to get involved.

'That's fine then, Chris,' says Mike. 'You'll be able to give us a few lessons.'

I have that same premonition of disaster that I had before we crashed the car. I mustn't get talked into this. 'What if Ralph's back next week?' I object.

'There's not much chance of that,' Mike answers. 'He's got a decent solicitor, but I don't think even he can get Ralph out of this one. They've got too much on him now.'

Trevor finishes off his pint. 'Anyway, Mike,' he says, 'this is going to take some thinking about.'

'Can we have your glasses, please, gentlemen?' The barman picks up Trevor's glass. It's after closing time.

'Shall we get together later in the week, then?' asks Trevor.

'O.K.' says Mike. 'How about Thursday?'

'That'll be all right. Is that O.K. for you, Chris?'

I don't know what to say to them. The plan is stupid, it won't work out and I don't want Sarah to get hurt. 'I don't know,' I say.

'Well, what night can you manage?'

I finish off my beer and take a deep breath. 'I'm not too keen on it,' I tell them. 'Can't you just leave me out of it?'

Trev and Mike glance at each other. There's an uncomfortable pause. 'Have you still got the keys to your dad's car?' Mike asks me suddenly.

I don't see what that's got to do with Mike's plan, but I'm pleased to change the subject. 'Yes.' I take the keys out of my pocket. 'I've got them here. I was thinking of posting them off somewhere . . .'

'Good idea,' says Mike. He picks up the empty crisp

packet from the table, opens it and shakes out the rest of the crumbs. 'Drop them in here,' he says, holding the packet open in front of me. 'I'll keep an eye on them.'

In the half second before I drop the keys into the bag, I notice Mike and Trevor exchanging glances. I realize that there's something wrong. I want to force myself to hesitate, to think about what I'm doing, but it's too late. My brain isn't working fast enough. By the time the message reaches my fingertips, the keys are already on their way down inside the bag. I don't know why I shouldn't hand over the keys; I just feel instinctively that it's wrong. And why did he ask me to drop them into the crisp packet? Why didn't he just pick them up himself?

Mike folds the crisp packet over and places it carefully in his pocket. Then he glances up at me. Across his face is the faint suggestion of a smile. 'Is your dad still upset about the car, then, Chris?' he asks.

Of course my dad's still upset. I can't understand why Mike's asking me. He's never shown any concern about it before. But there's something about the tone of his voice that makes me feel uncomfortable. I think he's implying something, but I don't know what. Maybe in the back of my mind I do know, but I just don't want to admit it.

'Time we were saying good-night, gentlemen,' hints the barman as he collects the rest of the glasses. I'll have to go soon or I'll miss the last bus.

I stand up ready to go. I shove my hands into the empty pockets of my jacket. I know I shouldn't have handed over the keys. They'll be covered in my fingerprints.

'We'll see you in here on Thursday, then, Chris,' says Mike.

I feel trapped. For the time being maybe, the safest thing I can do is say yes then try to get out of it later on.

'O.K.' I say to Mike. 'I'll see you on Thursday.'

'Right then, Chris.'
'Cheers.'
I walk out of the pub and down to the bus-stop.

24

A policeman comes to the door. He's seven foot tall and he looks like Trevor. 'We've found the body,' he tells my dad. My father nods his head in resignation. My mother weeps.

We drive down to the police station. Trevor takes off his helmet and sits in the driver's seat. I sit next to him with the corpse of Wishful Willy on my knee and my mother and father sitting silently in the back. The car cruises smoothly down the street.

We arrive at the police station and file inside. The desk sergeant lifts up the hinged part of the desk and ushers us past him towards the row of cells. On the stone wall is an elephant with a knot in its tail. 'Don't forget your keys,' it says. Trevor unhooks my father's car keys from the elephant's tail and uses them to open the cell.

Inside is a chapel of rest. The air is heavy with the scent of flowers. Against the rear wall is an altar. Lying in state on a marble block in the centre of the cell is the dismembered corpse of my father's G.T. San Marino. Wreaths of flowers lie across the bent front bumper. In the centre of the slab is the steering-wheel, snug and warm inside its hand-knitted glove. Close beside it, the gear-stick stands to attention, my father's initials monogrammed on to its cover. Behind the steering-wheel is the driver's seat on which my knitted jumper lies in state. On all the pieces of the car are fingerprints, black and inky, standing out as huge as lion's pawprints. Next to each fingerprint is a typewritten notice and an arrow, the sort they put on exhibits in a museum. I walk closer to read the notices. Each one says my name: Christopher Fieldsend.

I wake up feeling uneasy. I think I'm going to have to go back to the car.

I set off for school early but take a detour past the bus-stop. It's important that no one sees me. I ought to have an excuse ready, but I haven't been able to think of one. My mind isn't functioning too well.

I've left my fingerprints all over the car, my jumper inside it and I also moved the front seat forward. I could never pretend that anyone taller than me was driving it when it crashed. When Trevor wiped away the broken glass from the inside of the car, he would have wiped off his own fingerprints as well. I don't know whether that was deliberate or not. What I do know is that I have to go back to the scene of the crime and remove all the evidence I can.

It's a cold windy day and it's drizzling. I'm not sure how to reach the car. I could walk back up the hill to the place where we crashed it over the embankment and then try to climb down the steep drop into the valley. But that could be suicidal. If I fell, my body might lie unnoticed for days. I'll have to walk the long way round, following the path of the stream at the bottom of the valley. I turn up the collar of my jacket and plunge my hands deeply into my pockets. There's a long, cold walk ahead.

I turn off the road and begin to walk down the centre of the valley. The stream is dried-up now but it's muddy with the rain. Walking is difficult; it's going to take me longer than I thought. I feel alone and I feel afraid that the police could be there waiting for me, knowing I'm likely to return when I think of all the evidence I've left behind. I pause and stare up at the hillside. The trees and bushes are motionless.

I walk on. I know I'm vulnerable. The others in D.A.M.N. won't get blamed for the car, and it doesn't matter to them if the blame all falls on me. I feel betrayed. I wish there was someone I could talk to.

There is no proper path. My boots become caked with mud, and feel heavy and cumbersome. My legs feel as weak and brittle as a cockroach's, crawling through a treacle tin. What makes it worse is that the stream bed meanders to and fro like a strand of plaited hair; it's never straight. At every bend I slow down until I see that the way ahead is clear. The police could be waiting for me round every corner that I turn.

Suddenly, I hear a noise—a rustling as if there's someone hiding in the bushes. I stop and hold my breath. There's silence, apart from the pounding of my heart. I ease forward tentatively, straining my ears for any sound. The rustling's there again. I freeze. I haven't imagined it. I focus every pinpoint of my concentration on the bushes and trees in front of me, watching for any movement. A twig cracks. There's a definite movement now in the bushes; someone is crawling along behind them with a steady crunching of twigs and leaves. I'm starting to shake. I stand fixed to the spot. The noise becomes more distinct. Larger twigs crackle. I catch a glimpse of something brown, moving amongst the foliage. A ginger cat stalks out into the open. I close my eyes and breathe a long, drawn-out sigh.

I walk on more slowly, edging silently round the bushes at every bend in the path. I seem to have walked for miles. I begin to wonder if the car has been taken away somehow. I could be walking on for ever.

I'm just about to give up, when I see the car in front of me. I'm so pleased that I start to run towards it, eager to get the work done. I glance around briefly. I can't see anyone about.

The car looks almost intact; just squashed. It stares at me accusingly through its broken headlamps. The shattered windscreen looks the most painful, like a child who's had his glasses smashed in a fight. The door is swinging off its hinges like the policeman's broken arm.

I find my jumper inside the car and I use it to wipe round everywhere I touched: around the dashboard and the door handles—inside and outside the car. I sit on the driving seat then move it backwards as far as it will go, positioning it for someone about the size of Trevor. After that, I use my jumper to wipe around the seat lever. I think I've remembered everything. The only bad thing that happens is that I cut my leg. Kneeling on the car sill, I put my weight on a patch of jagged glass. The blood starts seeping straightaway into my jeans, but it doesn't hurt much.

When I've finished, I check that there's no one watching, then I stagger away with my jumper folded up inside my jacket. My knee's still bleeding, but I force myself to ignore it and try to run. When I've jogged along for a mile or so, I climb part way up the hillside and find a bramble bush. I bury the jumper deeply inside it. As I stumble back down the hill, I notice my footprints, a faint but definite line of them, wavering through the mud by the edge of the stream bed and returning on the other side. I hadn't noticed them before. I don't think it matters. There's nothing special or incriminating about my boots.

★

I arrive at school in time for lunch. I clean up my leg with a paper towel and, when it starts bleeding again, I go to the medical room and have it bandaged up. I tell them I've fallen down playing football in P.E.

25

Sarah is a beautiful queen imprisoned in a castle. I ride towards the castle on a large white horse, pounding through the forest, slashing my way through thickets. I scythe down guards with my rapier, then clamber up the winding staircase of the tower. I reach the top to a fanfare of trumpets and a thunder of applause. I swagger along the darkened passageway to her portal. I penetrate the room at the top of the tower and Sarah flings herself at my feet, her rescuer, her lord.

I alter my position. The sheets are wrinkled. I heave the duvet from the floor. I shuffle along the sheets into the cool, dry unslept-on side of the bed. The sheets behind me are damp and clammy.

Sarah has been arrested for giving out leaflets at the missile base. American soldiers have bundled her into a van. Sarah struggles. She attempts to escape. They tie her hands together with cords above her head and shove her roughly on to the floor. Sarah tries to stagger to her feet and make for the door. They strap her ankles together and leave her, locking the doors behind them.

The sound is that of erupting thunder. I sit astride my Harley Davidson one thousand c.c., silver and chrome reflecting in the sun, burning down the centre of the road. Behind me is a convoy of other, smaller bikes, straddling across the carriageway. I am their leader, resplendent in my silver-studded jacket. We halt at the missile base and regroup, petrol vapour shimmering in the air, bikes revving in anticipation as the riders await my orders. We will storm the van.

Under my instructions, the door to the van is battered. The gang have weakened it, but still the edges cling together. I grasp a nearby metal post and charge alone at the door, thrusting forward until the lock gives way and the metal crumples apart like tinfoil.

Sarah lies sobbing on the floor. As I stand astride her, the metal battering ram still heavy in my hands, she sinks back with relief and gratitude. Her rescuer, her lord.

I meet Sarah at the bus station to leaflet the bus queues. Since people have nothing to do, most of them accept the leaflets quite happily, then read through them before their buses arrive. 'Would you like to take a leaflet?' Sarah asks graciously, making it hard for people to refuse. Her whole manner is charming and polite.

'Thank you very much,' they say to her, as if they're honoured that Sarah has picked them out. I feel proud to be out with her; she's a star.

After about an hour, the bus station is almost deserted. 'Shall we go somewhere and have a cup of coffee?' Sarah suggests. 'We can give some more out later, when people start coming back into town.'

I had thought of that myself, but couldn't think where to suggest taking Sarah.

We go into a nearby café. It's grubby-looking and seedy, but Sarah doesn't seem to mind. We order some coffee.

'What about biscuits?' Sarah asks, peering over the counter.

'What have they got?'

'Well, there's a very difficult choice here. They've got chocolate digestives and . . . is that a Custard Cream I can see lurking down there? Yes, there are chocolate digestives, Custard Creams or . . .'

The joke clicks home. 'You can't see any Co-op shortcakes, can you?'

Sarah laughs. 'I think we'll have to put this to the vote.' She tries to sound serious. 'Now, all those in favour of chocolate digestives . . .'

'Ah, wait a minute—there are some people on very low incomes who might be offended at the price of chocolate biscuits . . .'

'On the other hand, we don't want people to think we do everything on the cheap . . .'

'Do you want serving or not?' The woman behind the counter's getting impatient.

'We're just trying to make our minds up,' I tell her.

'I can see that.'

'Shall we compromise on a packet of Rich Tea biscuits?' I suggest.

'To have with the coffee?'

'Why not?'

We take our coffee and biscuits over to a table in the corner and sit down.

I feel pleased at the way we both managed to laugh about the biscuits. Making a joke about the debate at the peace group is probably the easiest way of handling something that's a barrier between us otherwise. It's good to be able to share a joke with Sarah.

She stirs her coffee with a plastic teaspoon. There's silence for a little while.

'Look,' says Sarah, 'I hope Mike wasn't offended by

what I said to him in the pub. I thought afterwards that I might have gone over the top.'

I give a weak grin.

'He wasn't upset, was he?'

I nod. 'Very.'

'Oh dear.' Sarah sips some of her coffee. 'Perhaps I'd better apologize to him on Monday.'

My guts twist into a knot when I think about Mike's plan. I have to stop Sarah setting off for the meeting on Monday.

'Will your dad be coming to the meeting?' I ask her.

'No. He's away at a conference over the week-end. He won't be back until Tuesday. Why?'

I try not to show my disappointment. If Sarah were going to the meeting with her dad, then Mike's plan wouldn't work.

'I just thought he'd want to join in the discussion,' I tell her.

Sarah nods. 'I wouldn't want him to come anyway. Not with them trying to put me forward as Secretary.' She drinks some more of her coffee. 'He'd be tempted to speak up for me. It's important that I do things like that in my own right—not just as Bevan Barnforth's daughter.'

'I see.' I concentrate on stirring my coffee.

Sarah looks seriously at me. 'You don't want me to get elected, do you?' she asks. 'Aren't you more concerned about D.A.M.N. keeping in control?'

I shake my head. 'No.' I drink some coffee. It tastes of milk and chicory. 'I'm fed up with D.A.M.N.,' I say. 'I want to leave.'

'Why don't you?'

The reason that I can't leave D.A.M.N. is because of the car. They know that I'm the one who crashed it and they have the keys covered in my fingerprints. They could send those to the police, if they wanted to. I shrug my shoulders. There's no way I can explain this to Sarah. 'I will leave,' I tell her. 'I just haven't got round to it yet.'

Sarah doesn't look convinced.

I take a deep breath. 'I'm getting fed up with all these meetings, anyway,' I say to her. 'You wouldn't like to come to the cinema on Monday instead? There's a really good film on. I've been wanting to see it for ages.'

Sarah looks amazed. 'What is it?'

I struggle hard to think of what they were advertising for next week at the Odeon, when I passed it coming into town.

'*The Brides of Dracula*. I've seen all the others in the series. They're really good.'

Sarah laughs out loud. 'Oh, come on, Chris. You just don't want me to go to the meeting on Monday. You don't want me to get elected . . .'

'No, it's not that. I really want to see the film and I'll be busy in the week.'

'What about Sunday? Is it on then?'

'I don't know.'

'It must be. They change the films round on Sundays.' Sarah smiles at me and shakes her head. 'I would like to go to the pictures with you, Chris. I've never seen a Dracula film. Can't we go on Sunday?'

I nod my head in resignation.

'You don't seem very pleased.'

'No, that's fine.'

There's an uncomfortable silence. Sarah can tell that it isn't fine at all.

'What is it, then?'

I wish she wouldn't ask me. I feel this terrible longing to explain everything to Sarah; it's the way I felt when she telephoned me after the car crash. I want to break down and cry and have somebody to console me, to put their arms round me and hug me.

'What's the matter, Chris?'

I have to fight against it. I mustn't give anything away. 'Nothing,' I tell her. 'I'm O.K.'

I drink the rest of my coffee and leave most of the biscuits for Sarah. I don't feel like eating. 'Shall we give some more of the leaflets out?'

'O.K.'

We spend another half hour giving out leaflets, but people are only just trickling back into town. And, when they get off the buses, they're all in too much of a hurry to stop. We decide to give out the rest some other time.

My mother's kept my dinner warm in the oven. I don't feel very hungry, but I sit and try to eat something. My father walks into the kitchen and makes himself an extra cup of tea. 'Any news about the car?' I ask him.

'Not yet.' He sits down opposite me at the table and drinks his tea. 'I think we'll get it back though, you know. I was talking to Gordon about it last night at the Fellowship.'

That's the ex-servicemen's Fellowship my father goes to every month.

'Who's Gordon?'

'He used to be the Chairman of the Fellowship. Ex-C.I.D. chap.'

'Oh.'

'He's had plenty of experience with car thefts. He says the cars usually turn up not far from where they were taken . . .'

I cut tiny corners away from my sprouts to make it look

as if I'm eating them. I slice chunks off the meat and deftly hide them underneath my mashed potatoes.

'People often abandon stolen cars because they've run out of petrol. They often leave them in a bit of a mess, with all sorts of belongings lying around. That's how the C.I.D. usually find out who's responsible.'

'I see.'

My father shakes his head sadly. 'I don't know if I'd want to drive the car again, if I felt some stranger had been using it. I was thinking, I mean, it must be what a man would feel like if his wife had been . . .'

I look up at him. 'Been what?'

'You know . . . been . . . been with some other man.' He says this to me confidentially, man to man, as if my mother's ears might become contaminated from the sitting-room next door.

'Do you know what I mean?'

'Mmmmm . . . er . . . yes.'

'And they leave evidence behind . . . Apparently, the police find cigarette-ends and all sorts of obnoxious things on the back seats of stolen cars. They even find people's underwear. I mean, can you imagine driving your car again when you know that a pair of knickers belonging to a strange woman have been found underneath the back seat?'

I shake my head as I try again to tackle a boiled sprout.

'But, if it helps to find who the culprits are, I suppose it's all to the good. That's how we have to look at it.'

'Yes.'

'The main give-away of course is fingerprints. Apparently, thieves nearly always leave their fingerprints on a stolen car.'

I give up on the sprouts and look up at my father.

'Surely a professional car thief would always wipe his fingerprints away?'

He shakes his head knowingly. 'That's what Gordon was telling me,' he says. 'They try to, but there are always places that they miss. Where do you think police would look first for fingerprints on a stolen car?'

This is not a guessing game that I really want to play. I take a gulp of my tea. 'The door handles?' I suggest.

'No. Even an amateur thief would wipe those off.'

'The gear-stick? The steering-wheel?'

My father smiles and shakes his head, delighting in the confidential information.

'Go on, then. Where do they look?'

He puts down his cup of tea and leans towards me secretively. 'The first thing you'd do,' he confides, 'if you were driving a car that didn't belong to you, would probably be to alter the position of the driving seat. Right?'

'Right.'

'There might be some fingerprints on the seat catch, but they'd be difficult to pick up. The second thing you'd do would be to adjust the rear-view mirror. Everybody does that. They place their fingers on the chrome at the back of the mirror, leaving a beautiful set of fingerprints. That's the one place thieves never think of wiping afterwards.'

I start to feel faint. I picture myself sitting in the car, looking out through the jagged windscreen. Before I set off, I altered the rear-view mirror, which had been knocked out of place with the crash. I placed my fingers on the chrome. It felt cold to touch because I was hot and sweating. I positioned the mirror in such a way that I saw a full close-up of Trevor pushing the car. When I looked again later, Trevor was gone.

'Are you feeling all right, Christopher?'

I remember altering the mirror but, when I went back to the car, I know I didn't wipe it. My fingerprints will still be there, sleeping invisibly underneath the squashed roof, waiting to be matched with those that are on the set of keys.

'Christopher . . .?'

If they ever check up on me, I can't pretend I was at school that day. I wasn't marked present in the register and I never brought an absence note. The form teacher still keeps asking me for one. The only people who could give me an alibi are Mike, Trevor and Julie. I could admit I was with them at Bedgar and ask them to say that we all went there together in Ralph's van.

'Are you all right, Christopher?'

'Yes, I'm O.K., Dad. I'm fine.'

26

'Have you seen anything of Sarah this week, then, Chris?'

'Yes. I gave out leaflets with her yesterday.'

'Did she say whether her dad might be coming on Monday?'

'No, he won't. He's away at a conference over the week-end. He won't be back till Tuesday.'

'Very convenient.'

'We'll get this plan organized, then. I've checked out the road where Sarah lives and it's ideal. There are only three houses on it and one of them is definitely empty. There's a big overgrown garden with trees and plenty of cover. If you wait round there, Chris . . .'

I have to tell them. I can't leave it any longer. I place a hand on the edge of the table for support. 'Look,' I say, 'I'm not coming in on the plan.'

Mike stares hard at me. 'Why not?'

I take a deep breath. 'I've decided I want to leave D.A.M.N. I don't agree with it any more.'

Mike shakes his head, like a teacher talking to a kid who's given the wrong answer. 'You can't do that,' he says.

I feel a sense of panic. 'Why not?'

Mike counts out the reasons on his fingers. 'One—because you know too much about us; two—because you're going out with Sarah; three—well, you know the third one . . .' His face has a sarcastic ghost of a smile.

I think I know what the third reason is but I have to make sure. 'I *don't* know . . .'

Mike smiles at me openly. 'The car,' he says simply.

That was what I thought he meant. I hate him for being so sure.

'What's wrong with me seeing Sarah?' I object. 'I'm only doing what Ralph asked me to . . . I found out information. I told you about the vote and her dad being away next week. It's all been useful . . .'

Mike shakes his head. 'Ralph just told you to chat her up—not screw her.'

'I'm not . . .' I don't like to use an expression like that with regard to Sarah. 'It's not anything like that . . .'

'The way she was looking at you the other night, I thought you'd got some great love affair going on or something . . .'

I glare at Mike defiantly and say nothing.

Mike lights up two cigarettes and passes one to Trevor. He doesn't offer one to me.

'O.K., then,' says Trevor. 'We'd better get this thing organized. We haven't got that much time.'

'Right.' Mike takes a leaflet out of his pocket. On the back he draws a diagram of the street where Sarah lives. He draws little squares where the houses are. 'We'll be waiting for her when she leaves her house to come to the meeting. Right?'

'O.K.,' says Trev.

'She'll get dragged into the garden of this house over here . . .'

I can only think of one other thing to put them off. 'Look,' I say, 'one thing you haven't taken into account is the sort of person Sarah is. She's very strong-minded —very determined. You're basing this plan on the idea that, if she's really scared, she'll just give in. What if she doesn't agree to us beating this guy up—or pretending to beat him up—what's going to happen then? Do we just turn round and walk off home?'

'You mean . . .' Mike asks me, 'that Sarah's lying there about to get raped and, when we offer to work the guy over for her, she just says no . . . ?'

I shrug my shoulders. It doesn't sound likely but, knowing Sarah, there's a chance of that happening. 'That's right,' I answer. 'It's a possibility.'

Mike sneers. 'In that case,' he says, 'she'll just get what's coming to her.'

I gaze at him with loathing as he looks up at me challengingly, confident that I wouldn't dare to refute him. 'The rest of us can just stand back and fucking watch,' he says.

'Hello. Is that Sarah?'

'Hi, Chris. Nice to hear from you.'

'Listen. I need to talk to you.'

'Is it urgent?'

'Yes.'

'What's it about?'

'I can't explain over the phone.'

'Well, I'm busy tonight. Dad's having to rewrite the speech he's making at the conference and he's at a meeting now. I said I'd type it out for him . . .'

Pause.

'Will Saturday be O.K.?'

'I suppose so. What time?'

'Well, Helen's invited me to go riding with her in the afternoon. I'm going to their house afterwards. But that's quite near you. I mean, perhaps her dad could drop me off after tea . . . ?'

'O.K.'

I don't really want Sarah to see where I live, but I can't suggest anything else. 'Yes, that'll be all right. What time?'

'About seven?'

'O.K. That'll be fine.'

'I'll look forward to seeing you, then. Bye.'

'Good-bye, Sarah.'

I keep having nightmares on Friday night. I go downstairs and make myself a cup of tea, and when I go back to bed I try to think about what I ought to say to Sarah. But my thoughts refuse to be focused into words. They parade through my head as a montage of scenes and voices, none of them making sense.

Mike's face, grinning at me sarcastically, appears in massive close-up, but his huge, hairy hands are Trevor's, paying out a chain that's like a werewolf's lead. I see Trevor lifting up the Mini-van as if it's a cardboard cut-out; hanging out of the window is a policeman's arm, mis-shapen as a dead frog's leg and clinging hold of a jumper that has my mother's knitting needles stuck in it still.

I see a police dog, sniffing at a trail of blood, tracking through the mud towards a hillside. A policeman with a blood-stained, battered face removes the bandage from my leg. 'But you don't play football, do you . . . ?' he says to me. 'Chess is more your game.'

I see Donna Massey's long and suntanned thighs, stretched out leisurely underneath the table as she moves a white knight forward. And I am a white knight, galloping onwards to rescue Sarah, charging forwards to carry her to safety. But Sarah stands frozen in terror. She stares at me in disbelief. 'No . . .' she screams. 'No! No!!!'

I become Sarah as she confronts the darkened figure, emerging out of the shadows. I see the horror-mask, crinkled and rubbery, the bulging eyes and scarred, mis-shapen face. I remember Sarah telling me that you have to ignore the uniform and concentrate on what the man is like inside . . .

27

I get washed and changed before Sarah comes and then I go down to the paper shop and buy some cigarettes. When I come back, I have to get washed and changed again because my shirt is soaked with sweat. I sit on my bed and smoke the cigarettes and then I start pacing up and down, watching out of the window for Mr Wheatley's car. I see the Rover drawing up outside. Sarah climbs out and waves to Mr Wheatley as he drives away.

I grab my jacket and walk downstairs to meet her on the drive. Sarah looks surprised that I'm not inviting her into the house, but I can't bear the thought of introducing her to my parents. Letting her see where I live is bad enough.

'Shall we go for a walk?' I ask her.

'All right.'

As Sarah turns, she looks at the garden and I can see her trying to distinguish the shape of the gnomes in the darkness. She stares incredulously, then turns as if she's about to ask me something.

'Come on.' I put my arm on her shoulder and steer her away towards the street.

I'd like to keep my arm around her, but I don't. I let it fall to my side and we walk a little way apart. Sarah tries to make conversation by talking about the leaflets and asking when we should give the others out, but I only answer in monosyllables. I don't want to chat about leaflets.

We walk along the empty streets and I wish that Sarah was my proper girlfriend and we were walking together arm-in-arm, laughing and chatting and pausing and kissing each other. I wish that D.A.M.N. and the nuclear bomb were a thousand light years away.

We walk to the edge of the housing estate to the place the kids all call the Rec. The children's recreation ground. We wander inside and I lead Sarah towards the graffiti-covered shelter where there's a carved-up wooden bench. We sit down together and stare at the ghostly shapes of the stationary swings and hibernating rocking-horses. All Sarah's attempts at easy chat have failed. The silence is overpowering.

'What did you want to talk to me about?' she asks at last.

I light up a cigarette and throw the match away. I wish I had never belonged to D.A.M.N. I wish I'd met Sarah before I'd had anything to do with them. I don't see how I can explain to her about the plan and I don't know how to tell her that I love her.

'It did sound urgent on the phone,' she says and places her hand on my arm.

I inhale on my cigarette and stare straight ahead at the swing frame. The chains on the swings begin to creak gently in the breeze.

'It's about the meeting on Monday,' I say at last.

Sarah waits for me to continue. The chains make an eerie, whimpering sound.

'I don't want you to go.'

There's a pause. 'Why not?'

I can't explain to her. I shake my head.

'Well, there must be a reason. Isn't it what I said before—you don't want me to be elected because you don't want D.A.M.N. to lose control?'

I shake my head again.

'Come on, Chris. You'll have to explain it better than that.'

Sarah's voice is soft and coaxing. She wants me to be open and honest with her. I think she's genuinely concerned that I'm upset. I just don't see how I can explain to her about the plan. 'Mike and Trev have got something organized,' I tell her. 'It would be safer if you stayed at home. They want to stop you being elected.'

'But that's ridiculous. I'm only speaking for the majority of members. If I didn't oppose them, someone else would. There would have to be re-elections some time.' Sarah pauses, thinking. 'Anyway,' she asks uneasily, 'you said *safer*. What did you mean? Why would it be *safer* if I didn't go?'

If I described all the details of the plan to her, she would probably tell her father and he'd go to the police. Mike and Trevor would no doubt find a way of putting the blame for this one on to me as well. What I have to do is make Sarah trust me and accept that she mustn't go to the meeting, without my having to explain to her why not.

'Just because you disagree with another person's ideas, it doesn't make you hate them.' Sarah stares thoughtfully at the swing frames. 'None of them would harm me.'

'They're very violent—especially Mike. I saw him at the riot in Bedgar. Please don't go to the meeting, Sarah.'

Sarah frowns. 'But, how could they harm me at a public meeting? What are they planning to do?'

'I can't explain.'

'You mean you *won't* explain?'

I nod.

Sarah rests her chin in her hands and stares ahead.

'You say you don't agree with D.A.M.N.,' she says, 'but you obviously feel loyal to them . . .'

I don't answer her. I smoke my cigarette.

'I know what I'll do,' she says decisively. 'I'll apologize to Mike straightaway. I could phone him up and say I think I went too far with what I said to him the other night. I won't tell him I didn't mean what I said, because I think it's true, but . . .'

'It's too late for that,' I interrupt. 'Mike's not just angry about what you said the other night—there are other reasons as well . . .'

'Like what?'

I hesitate. I understand why Mike dislikes Sarah so much, but it's not easy to put it into words. 'It's like what you were saying about policemen. You talked about hating a uniform when you don't even know the man inside. Mike doesn't hate you as a person because he doesn't even know you properly, but he hates the things you stand for . . .'

'What sort of things?'

I don't want to offend Sarah, but I have to make her understand. 'I think he sees you as an extension of your father—someone who's rich and clever and successful, all the things he'd like to be. And, as well as that, he finds you attractive . . .'

Sarah nods and listens. 'Don't you want me to tell Mike you've been talking to me about Monday?' she asks.

'No.'

'That's loyalty again, isn't it?' Sarah takes a deep breath. 'You were loyal enough to tell them about the meeting at our house. How else did they find out about me standing for Secretary?'

The answer is obvious, but I can't bring myself to admit it to her.

Sarah sighs deeply. 'Your relationship with D.A.M.N. seems to be more important than your relationship with anyone else,' she says.

'Look, Sarah,' I explain. My voice is rising with emotion now. I'm really frightened that I'm just not getting through to her. 'It's extremely important that you stay away from the meeting on Monday. I can't tell you what D.A.M.N. have organized, but it's nasty and I don't want you to get hurt.'

Sarah just stares downwards, scraping the heel of her boot around in circles.

I take a deep breath. 'I care a lot about you, Sarah. I can't bear the thought of you getting hurt.'

Still Sarah doesn't respond.

'Because I know people in D.A.M.N., I'm the only one who can protect you. I want to do that, Sarah. I want to look after you. That's much more important to me than any loyalty I might once have felt for D.A.M.N. . . .'

I wish Sarah would cry. If she were overcome with

emotion, leaning on me for support, I could handle this scene a lot better.

I reach inside me to draw on the strength I need to tell her the thing that's most important. 'I love you, Sarah,' I say at last.

I pause, waiting for Sarah to respond. I want to touch her, to hold her, to put my arms around her. I want her to tell me that she loves me in return. I have this horrible feeling that I'm the one who's going to cry.

Sarah still stares down at the ground, scraping her heel backwards and forwards, wiping away toffee papers and spent matchsticks . . . 'How do I know you're not making it all up?' she asks. 'All this could just be an elaborate ploy to keep me at home on Monday . . .'

I feel shocked that she doesn't believe me. 'I wouldn't make it up,' I tell her.

'You just think I ought to trust you . . .'

'Yes.' I finish my cigarette. 'Why not?'

Sarah sighs again then sits and thinks for a moment. 'I did . . .' she hesitates . . . 'I did think before that . . . that we might be able to share a relationship with each other. And actually . . . I thought we could get on well together. I found myself becoming . . . becoming quite fond of you.' She turns her head and looks at me. 'What I was afraid of was that you were using me . . . that you weren't really interested in me as a person, just as someone to convert to your campaign. A lot of things you've said have reinforced that . . .'

'What things?'

'Telling the others in D.A.M.N. about the vote of no-confidence and my name being put forward as the new Secretary; not wanting me to let Mike know about this conversation with you; not telling me the details about this plan they've got organized . . .'

I wish that Sarah would put her arms around me and bury her head in my jacket. I wish that she'd be frightened, needing me, relying on me.

'I do care about you, Sarah,' I tell her. 'I haven't been trying to convert you. In fact, I think it's worked the other way round: you're the one who's converted me.'

Sarah smiles and looks more relaxed. She reaches across and takes hold of my hand. We sit a while in silence, holding hands like a pair of lost children in the playground. 'I'm sorry,' Sarah says at last. 'I should have trusted you more.'

Her head is bent. I let go of her hand and hold it with my other, and then I gently stroke her hair. I bend down and kiss her hair. My chest feels tight and my eyes are beginning to swell with tears. I sniff. My breath is heavy with her perfume and the texture of her hair. It touches me deeply to think of Sarah trusting me. I don't think Sarah's going to tell me that she loves me, but I think this is going to be the beginning of our relationship, not the end. That's the most important thing. I squeeze Sarah's hand tightly.

Sarah looks up at me, then lifts my hand towards her lips and kisses my fingers.

'You want to carry on seeing me?' she asks.

I nod. I don't know how she could doubt it.

'Well . . .' she says thoughtfully . . . 'if what you said about your attitude to D.A.M.N. is true, then you're not going to be involved at all in this plan . . .'

I don't know if that's a question or not, but I don't answer.

'. . . and you can stop it happening by threatening to tell me or threatening to go to the police.' Sarah pauses, thinking deeply. 'I don't let anyone intimidate me,' she goes on, 'and I'm not afraid of Mike or Trevor or anyone else . . . I'll still go to the meeting on Monday, Chris, but I'll trust you and rely on you to make sure that I'm O.K.'

28

The phone rings.
'Hi.'
'Hello. Can I speak to Chris, please?'
Why doesn't she recognize my voice? 'This is Chris.'
'It's Sarah.'
'I know.'

A voice from the kitchen. 'Christopher . . . ?'
'Coming in a minute.'

I can hear the sound of Sarah breathing. 'Did you ask them about it?'
'Yes.' Silence. 'They wouldn't take any notice of me.'
'What do you mean?'
'They wouldn't listen to me.'

'Can you come here, please, Christopher . . . ?'
'Just a minute.'

'Look, Sarah, you'll have to stay at home tomorrow night. The meeting's not important. You can get someone else to speak instead of you. They can have the vote some other time . . .'
'It's a matter of principle, Chris. I'm not going to let them scare me off like that.'

'Christopher, there's a man from the C.I.D.'

'I'm coming.'
'He says they've found the car.'
My stomach sinks like a cannonball. I clutch hold of the telephone for support.

Sarah carries on speaking. 'I'll talk to them about it. I'll speak to Mike.' Her voice is firm and adamant.

I can't face the C.I.D. I don't know what to do.

'Did you hear what I said, Chris . . . ?'
Silence.
'I said I'd speak to Mike about it.'
'No.' I start to panic. 'Don't do that.'
'Why not? I'm not letting them play stupid games with me. If they won't listen to you, then I'll have to talk to them.'
'Please Sarah . . .' I try to make myself keep calm. I try to gather my thoughts together. 'Please don't. Just leave it to me. I'll look after you. I'll come round to see you on Monday, if you like. We could go out somewhere together . . .'
'Aren't we going out tonight, now?'
Pause. 'No.'

My father comes into the hall. 'Please hurry up, Christopher. He wants to take all our fingerprints . . .'
'I won't be long.'

'Look, Chris, I don't just want to try and avoid the situation. If it means a direct confrontation, then we'll have to have one. I won't let them intimidate me.'
I cup my hand around the telephone and lower my voice. I don't know whether my father's listening or not. 'Please don't talk to Mike, Sarah. There's something I need him to do for me. I can't fall out with him . . .'

211

'And what I think doesn't matter, does it?'

'No, I . . .'

'I'll let you know what happens. Good-bye, Chris.'

She puts down the telephone.

I force myself to smile at the detective, but I wish my lips would stop trembling. I try to make myself look pleased that they've found the car. I pull out a chair and sit down to stop myself collapsing into a heap upon the floor. 'Where did you find it?' I ask. I can't understand why my voice sounds two octaves higher than normal.

The detective looks at me curiously. 'Old Harrow Gorge,' he says.

'Never heard of it,' I squeak. 'I've never been there.' I wonder if I've spoken too quickly. I've not been charged with anything yet.

I need to show more enthusiasm about the car. 'How will you . . .' I clear my throat and bring my voice nearer normal. 'How will you lift it out?' I ask, trying to look interested. 'Do you have a special crane?'

'Isn't the car still roadworthy, then?' my father asks. 'You didn't say it was at the *bottom* of the gorge.'

The detective stares at me with definite suspicion. 'I was just about to tell you,' he says to my father. 'It's a complete write-off.'

'Just let your hand relax,' the detective tells me, as he lifts up my finger to place it in the ink-pad.

I grin at him stupidly. My hand is shaking like the wing of a squashed butterfly. I gaze at the duplicated sheet with the boxes drawn and labelled ready for the blotches of ink that will seal my fate for ever.

The detective rolls my fingertip across the ink, then lifts it up and places it on the paper in the first, neatly-drawn box. He takes the prints of each finger separately, then all my fingers together, first one hand, then the other. Then two prints of my thumbs together. It takes quite a long time.

'Is there any evidence with the car?' my father asks whilst he's waiting. 'Was there anything left inside it apart from fingerprints?'

'Oh, yes. They always leave something. Just little bits and pieces—nothing that most people would notice. There's blood around the bottom of the door, there are footprints all over the ground near where it crashed . . . I think we'll soon find who was responsible.'

'Well, I hope you get him locked up,' my father says. 'People like that need to be put away.'

The phone keeps on ringing, but Sarah doesn't answer. I'm certain she's at home. I try again, persistently, allowing the phone to ring and ring—my voice shouting out for Sarah to talk to me, echoing unanswered through the rooms of her house. I put down the phone then try again, five seconds later, two minutes later, a quarter of an hour . . .

She leaves the phone off the hook. All I hear is the engaged tone.

At quarter to seven, I go round to her house. I know she doesn't want to see me, but I have to talk to her.

It's a long time before Sarah answers the door. I stand waiting, conscious of the fact that she might be watching me from somewhere, peering behind the curtains, hoping that I'll go away. I ring the bell again. After a couple of minutes, I hear footsteps and Sarah opens the door. She looks harassed and upset. Her eyes are red as if she's been crying. 'I don't want to see you any more,' she says.

'I've got to talk to you.'

She stands and glares at me. She looks angry and hurt.

'I've got to talk to you,' I repeat.

We look at each other for a few seconds. Sarah doesn't stand aside. After a while, I simply enter the house and walk past her. I go into the kitchen. Sarah follows. We stand in the kitchen, facing each other. 'I'd prefer you to leave me alone,' she says.

'I've got to talk to you, Sarah.'

I walk towards her and gently place my arm on her shoulder but she shrugs me away. She moves across to a chair at the other end of the long kitchen table. She sits down and rests her chin in her hands.

'Did you phone Mike?' I ask her.

Sarah closes her eyes for a moment and nods her head in resignation.

'What did he say?'

Sarah sighs heavily. When she speaks, she looks downwards, addressing her words to the bleached, wooden surface of the table. 'I told him that I'd spoken to you and realized that there was something happening tomorrow that you were worried about. I said you didn't want to tell me, so I was asking him about it. And I apologized for upsetting him the other night . . .'

'What did he say about it?' I pull out a chair at the other end of the table and sit down. Sarah hasn't invited me to stay, but it seems harder to talk to her when I'm standing up.

Sarah looks up at me and her eyes are full of hurt. 'He said that you were conning me. He said that's what they'd arranged for you to do to keep me at home tomorrow night so I wouldn't be elected. He wouldn't have told me, he said, if it wasn't for the fact that I'd just apologized to him.'

'It's not true, Sarah.'

'I told him I didn't believe it. I said I thought that you were straight and honest and that . . . that you seemed to be growing quite fond of me and you wouldn't do a thing like that.'

I nod my head slowly to show that what she says is right.

'But Mike said,' Sarah hesitates, as though it's painful for her to have to talk about all this, 'he said that's what they'd set up right from the start. That's why Ralph asked me to work on the leaflet with you . . . so that you could come round here and . . . *chat me up* he said.'

'It's not true, Sarah.'

I have to try and make her understand. 'I do care about you,' I tell her. 'You've got to trust me. I want to look after you and protect you. You've got to let me do that . . .'

Sarah looks at me coldly. 'Is that what you want?' she asks. 'It makes you feel chivalrous to think I'm weaker than you and need protecting . . . ?'

I don't see what's wrong with that. 'Yes,' I tell her.

Sarah looks directly at me and her eyes are hard and unyielding. 'That's not the kind of relationship I ever want to have,' she tells me. 'Not with anybody.'

She pauses, running her hand across the surface of the wood. 'My friendships have to be on an equal basis,' she says. 'I'm not going to pretend to be weak and frail and stupid just because it makes it easier for someone to relate to me like that.'

'But you can't look after yourself tomorrow, Sarah. You'll get hurt.'

'I'm not pretending to be physically very strong, so it hardly seems possible that men like Mike or Trevor could attack me. How could they hurt someone who offers no resistance—who's physically incapable of fighting back?'

I don't answer.

'How would they feel?' she asks me. 'How would *you*

feel?' She doesn't give me time to think. 'There's no way people can ever win in that situation—when there isn't any opposition.' She pauses for a moment. 'I realize I could get hurt,' she goes on, 'but that's a risk I'm prepared to take. They're the ones who'll feel worse about it afterwards. I'd still win through in the end.'

I start to realize, with growing horror, that there's nothing I can say that will dissuade her. 'I think you're being stupid,' is all I can say. 'I've offered to do what I can to help you. If you're just too proud to accept that, then there's nothing else that I can do.'

'It's not pride,' says Sarah, 'that prevents me from entering into relationships based on the notion that I'm weak and need protecting. I'm as competent and clever as you are—more so, probably. If I ever meet someone who's prepared to accept that about me, then I might think about having some relationship with him.'

I don't know what to say to that. I start to feel angry and resentful.

Sarah's voice is scornful and bitter. 'You and I are a thousand miles apart, Chris,' she says slowly. 'You've been brought up in a world of male superiority, status symbols and garden gnomes.' She looks scathingly at my jacket. 'Studded jackets are a part of it, rescuing women in distress is part of it, and it's the world that's made the Bomb. I haven't been brought up as part of that world, but I'm prepared to spend my life fighting against it.'

She sighs deeply. 'That's the world where you belong, Chris. I don't want you round here any more.'

I feel frustrated that I haven't been able to get through to Sarah, but I feel deeply angry as well that she's criticizing things she doesn't understand. Not just criticizing me; but rejecting me. Saying I'm not good enough for her. I hate her for it. I could hit her.

We stare at each other for a few seconds. Who does she think she is? What right has she got to criticize me?

'Go away, Chris. Take your studded jacket and your chauvinism with you; go back to playing soldiers and army with the other overgrown kids in D.A.M.N. But leave us free to organize the campaign against nuclear missiles. Just get off our backs and leave us to get on with it. We haven't got that much time left.'

I stand and stare at her. I can't think of anything else to say. I turn around and walk out of the door.

29

I want to destroy her. Sarah is the only girl I've ever loved and now the dream has gone. I feel once more as though I came so near to touching something completely above and beyond myself, some new high level of experience, some peak I might not glimpse again, that I can hardly bear to admit to myself that the experience I've been aching for has now been lost for ever.

The more I think about Sarah and what she said to me, the more angry I become. I feel the rage building up inside me, strangling in my throat, burning into my eyes and threading its way along my guts.

I want to destroy her. I don't want her to win: that's the thought I keep uppermost in my mind. I want her to feel humiliated.

I walk down towards the garden of the empty derelict house where the carrier-bag will be waiting for me. I walk down the centre of the unpaved road, knowing there will be no traffic. It's turning dusk now and the sun is casting long, low shadows. The air is quiet except for the singing of birds. On either side of me the trees grow tall and heavy with a canopy of leaves that are just beginning to turn gold. The road is so peaceful and calm and enclosed that it's almost like entering a church. It's like a kind of sanctuary.

It's quite a long street, considering it only has three houses. I turn and walk through the iron gates with the padlock that's been smashed apart. As I push the gate, it creaks with a sound like someone crying.

The carrier-bag has been hidden in the bushes where we arranged. I kneel down on the uncut grass and tip out the contents: an old grey anorak, a pair of gloves, a mask. I spread them out on the grass. It's early yet, so I sit down and light a cigarette. I press the button on my watch, fifteen minutes still to go. I inhale on the cigarette and try to make myself relax, but all I can feel is hatred.

I think back to the dream I had about rescuing Sarah —riding on the white horse, penetrating the castle. I saw myself as a white knight and Sarah as a queen. The game has changed now; the dream has gone. The white knight takes the queen.

I smoke on the cigarette and cast my mind over the plan. I felt nervous about it before, but now I feel calm and more resolute, conscious of the mission, assured that what I have to do is right and necessary.

I take off my jacket, fold it up, then place it on the grass beside me. As I do so, my hand touches something soft and frail and brittle. I turn and look. Beside me, lying almost hidden in the grass, is the body of a baby bird: a sparrow, freshly dead. I pick it up and sling it across towards the gate, then I wipe my hand on the outside of the anorak.

I put the anorak on. It's too large for me and smells musty and unfamiliar. I fasten the zip on the front, then pick up my cigarette.

I sit smoking with my jacket folded next to me. I run my hand along the familiar worn black leather, then trace my fingers over the silver heads of the three-sided metal studs. They feel cold and hard to touch. I don't want to leave the jacket here behind me. The jacket is an important part of me and I hate Sarah for the way she sneered at it. *Take your jacket with you*, she said. I cling hold of it protectively.

The jacket is me. I am the jacket. It has the initials of my group on it: D.A.M.N. Like Sarah said, I belong to them; they own me.

I stub out my cigarette on the patch of grass in which I found the body of the baby bird.

I think of the white knight moving forward to take the queen and I start to relish the power of winning. I despise Sarah for rejecting me and making me feel humiliated. I want to destroy her. I like watching other people know they're beaten.

I put the mask on, calm and cool; then the gloves. I want to see the look of horror on her face.

I pick up my jacket again from the ground. I can feel the studs beneath the thickness of my glove. D.A.M.N.—the group I belong to, the group that controls me. The enormous power moving me, carrying me forward—huge magnetic forces shifting me into position like a pawn pulsating on an electronic chess board. All I can do is stand in front of the force and tremble, the way I stood on the stage at the Civic Hall, shaking at the unleashed powers of the crowd.

I take off the mask. It looks repulsive. I take off the gloves and lay them down beside me. Then I unzip the musty anorak, take it off and place it inside the carrier-bag. I pick up my own jacket and put it on, running my hand along the familiar worn black leather. I don't want to act this scene as a pawn for D.A.M.N. I don't want to be the pawn that goes forward and takes the queen because then she brings the castle into play, trapping me, defeating me. I want to act this scene for myself.

I put the mask back on and then I check my watch again. It's time to go. I zip up my jacket, then stand up, pulling on the gloves.

I know that what Sarah said is true: you can't win when there isn't any opposition; you can't score any victories over someone who refuses to fight. Sarah would never allow herself to be used. She has principles that she sticks to, that she'll never compromise upon. No matter how upset or frightened she is, she'll stick by what she believes in. What she said to me is true. Sarah is stronger and cleverer than me. She's the one who'll win through in the end.

Fuck Sarah.

I walk towards the gate with the broken padlock, past the body of the baby bird. I kick it out of the way with the heel of my boot. As I push open the gate, it creaks with a sound like someone crying, a soft whimper like the voice of a woman or a child.

The road is peaceful and calm and enclosed. It's like entering a sanctuary.

I wear the mask and gloves, but my own jacket as I walk down the street to meet Sarah.

OTHER PAPERBACK ORIGINALS

Bad Apple Larry Bograd
The Horribles Go for Broke Michael de Larrabeiti
Dance on my Grave Aidan Chambers
Dear Comrade Frances Thomas
The Firelings Carol Kendall
The Girl with a Voice Peggy Woodford
I Love You, Stupid! Harry Mazer
Lizzie's Floating Shop John Wain
A Proper Little Nooryeff Jean Ure
If It Weren't For Sebastian . . . Jean Ure
Rainbows of the Gutter Rukshana Smith
Sumitra's Story Rukshana Smith
To Be Looked For Timothy Ireland
Tunes for a Small Harmonica Barbara Wersba
Your Friend, Rebecca Linda Hoy